Screen Printing Primer

Second Edition

by Samuel T. Ingram

GATF*Press*
Pittsburgh

GATF*Press*   **Orders to:**
Graphic Arts Technical Foundation   GATF Orders
200 Deer Run Road   P.O. Box 1020
Sewickley, PA 15143-2600   Sewickley, PA 15143-1020
Phone: 412/741-6860   Phone (U.S. and Canada): 800/662-3916
Fax: 412/741-2311   Phone (all other countries): 412/741-5733
Email: info@gatf.org   Fax: 412/741-0609
Internet: http://www.gatf.org   Email: gatforders@abdintl.com

TABLE OF CONTENTS

FOREWORD

A crash course in screen printing? Yes, that's what we have asked of Sam Ingram, Professor of Graphic Communications at Clemson University. This book offers a short, illustrated, non-technical orientation to the field along with a glossary of basic terms.

The aim of the GATF*Press* primer series is to communicate the essential concepts of printing processes and technologies. Other primers focus on lithography, flexography, gravure printing, on-demand and digital printing, and computer-to-plate, and new titles are being planned.

Screen Printing Primer is useful to students, graphic artists, print buyers, publishers, salespeople in the graphic communications industry—to anyone who would like to know more about the printing process.

GATF*Press* is committed to serving the graphic communications community as a leading publisher of technical information. Please visit the GATF website at http://www.gatf.org for additional information about our resources and services.

Peter Oresick
Director
GATF*Press*

PREFACE

All printing processes visually communicate ideas, whether as text, images, or a combination of the two. As a manufacturing process, printing may create, decorate, or enhance products. The screen printing process demonstrates simplicity and complexity, art and science, small and large.

In simple terms, screen printing offers perhaps the most diverse printing option currently used in manufacturing. Screen printing has a rich history of graphic applications: wall coverings, clothing, and furniture were typically decorated by screen printing. Today's screen printing industry ranges in applications from membrane switch technology to fine art to textile and garment products. Technological innovation has continued to integrate quality and responsiveness to the industry. Large-format graphics, container printing, and use of nonconventional ink systems are but a sampling of the product options readily available via screen printing.

Screen printing also offers the versatility to apply graphics and materials to practically any shape, composition, or number of substrates. Versatility is a notable attribute of screen printing, but other characteristics enhance the process as well. Screen printing can transfer variable thicknesses of ink, adding value to products requiring weatherability, lightfastness, and resistance to aggressive materials.

How does the process work? Simply stated, it is a through-transfer process. The ink is pushed through an open-weave screen fabric, which is coated in nonimage areas to prevent ink from passing through. The open areas of the fabric pass ink to reproduce the image. Printing of this nature is typically described as stencil printing.

Although screen printing commands a small share of the total print market, no other process can claim applications as far ranging. An overview of the manufacturing segments provides insight concerning this point. Garment and textile printing involves decorating both assembled clothing and cloth materials, which will be further processed. Decal printing includes product identification, ceramics, decorations, and short-term product displays. The electronics industry uses screen printing for membrane switches, solder masks, and circuit boards. Display graphics offers point-of-purchase and various signage products. Outdoor advertising ranges from fleet marking to billboards. Container printing incorporates screen printing on toner cartridges, cups, and lighters among the numerous container products decorated. Art and commercial screen printing produce fine art reproductions, serigraphs, and variations from postcards to calendars to posters.

Materials that may be printed or decorated by screen printing are presumably endless. Ink manufacturers supply products for screen printers with concern for adhesion, color fidelity, durability, lightfastness, and many other attributes that address the gamut of material applications found in screen printing. Press manufacturers design machines ranging from tabletop sizes to press beds that measure over 30 ft. (10 m). Presses may consist of one print unit or in-line configurations of 16 units. Employees in an operation may consist of a single individual producing a sole product line. Another plant may produce entire product lines and involve hundreds of people.

Diversity, flexibility, quality, uniqueness. These are but a few of the terms that define screen printing's role in the graphic communications industry. This book offers insight into the industry, the process, and the components that combine to highlight screen printing as a manufacturing process responsive to consumer needs. I trust you will find this book helpful in understanding how the screen printing process differentiates product and application.

Sam Ingram
July 1998
Clemson University

For my family, Marilyn, Katie, and Emily,
who have shown love and enthusiasm for my desire to learn.
Thanks to my colleagues and the students
who have provided me with much to learn.

1 THE PRINTING PROCESSES

Before one can understand the bases for competition among the printing processes there must be a clear understanding of their concepts. *Printing processes* are mechanical ways of transferring ink or toner images onto the surfaces of the materials being printed, called *substrates*. The principles applied to separate the image from the nonimage areas in each process are key to the rest of the story, so this is where we will begin.

SCREEN PRINTING

Screen printing, still known by too many as "silk screening," is a stencil process wherein the image area is open and the nonimage area is closed. Ink is moved through the stencil by a resilient squeegee. The stencil/plate is most commonly made from a light-sensitive emulsion, photographically imaged so the areas to print are washed away while the nonimage areas are made permanent. The stencil is processed on a fine fabric, most commonly polyester, which holds the parts of the design in place. Without the screen fabric, there would be a problem holding the centers of letters such as D, P, and A in position. Ink is transferred through the open stencil and mesh onto the substrate. Figure 1-1 shows the key parts of the screen printing system.

Screen printing permits the control of ink film thickness by the diameter of the fibers that form the mesh. It is capable of applying very thick ink films, a strength. It is, however, limited in how thin a film of ink it can produce. It is widely used in the highest quality of packaging labels and in outdoor advertising where qualities includ-

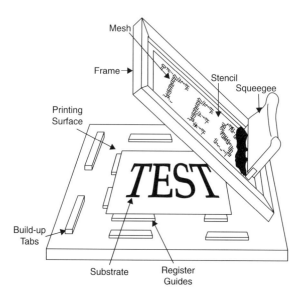

Figure 1-1. Schematic of the screen printing process.

ing long life and continuous resistance to the elements are required. Its thick ink film provides more pigment deposit, which facilitates great durability. It is routinely found in both flatbed and rotary applications. It is commonly used in-line with other processes where its thick ink film is desired for visual and/or tactile appeal or for protection, as in applications of clear coatings over other printing.

Screen printing accounts for an estimated 3%* ($41.4–$68.1 billion) of graphics printing. Screen printing is also a major industrial process used in imaging dials and gages; production of gaskets; glass, ceramic, and metal decoration; and electrical and electronic switches, circuits, and component manufacturing.

LETTERPRESS AND FLEXOGRAPHY

Letterpress, the original printing method, is a *relief* process. The printing plate is hard; it has a reverse-reading image raised above

---

* *Statistics of print market shares for the various processes are from Mike Bruno's What's New(s) in Graphic Communications, No. 129 (July–August 1997)*

the nonimage area. When rollers carrying an even and thin coat of paste ink are rolled over the surface, the only part of the plate to receive ink is the raised "face" of the image. This inked image is immediately impressed against the substrate (the material being printed), creating a right-reading reproduction. Figure 1-2 illustrates the plate and the way it transfers ink to a substrate.

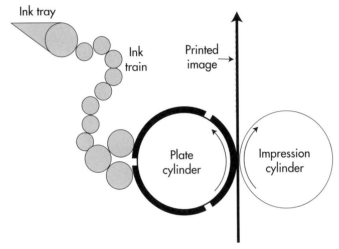

Figure 1-2. Schematic of the letterpress printing process.

The hard letterpress plate is either made of metal, usually magnesium, or photopolymer. Modern applications are most commonly on web (rollfed) presses where the plate is wrapped around a cylinder. Letterpress requires a roller train, series of rollers, to work the heavy paste ink into a semi-liquid, uniform film for transfer to the plate. This roller train system has many moving parts and requires proper adjustment and maintenance to perform at a high-quality level. Because the plate is hard, it only produces high quality on very smooth surfaces, thus not being very useful for a multitude of porous, irregular substrates. Narrow-web letterpresses, the ones most commonly found in competition with flexo, use ultraviolet (UV) curing inks in order to achieve any reasonable production speed. These require expensive curing units on each print unit.

This makes letterpress an expensive alternative, still limited to the smoothest of substrates, when compared to flexo. It is estimated that 7% of printing is currently done by letterpress.

Flexography is another relief process similar to letterpress. Relief, however, is where the similarities end. The flexo plate is resilient instead of hard like letterpress. The flexographic ink is a liquid instead of paste. And the inking system is simple; it is a gravure cylinder called an *anilox roll.* The anilox roll is inked, wiped clean (usually with a doctor blade). and printed onto the raised image area of the resilient plate. The ink remains wet long enough to transfer to the substrate. Because the plate is resilient, made of rubber or photopolymer, it can be impressed against the widest variety of surfaces and print without voids, snowflakes. According to the Flexographic Technical Association, over 25% of printing is produced by the flexographic process. Figure 1-3 provides a diagram of the simple flexo print station.

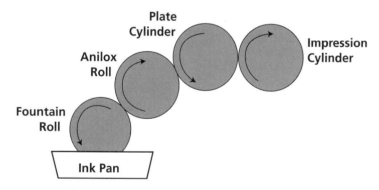

Figure 1-3. Schematic of the flexographic print station.

LITHOGRAPHY

Offset lithography is the leading process (estimated to be 40%) in total dollar volume of printing and dominates general commercial printing markets. The plate is flat and the image area is separated from nonimage areas by its chemical difference. The right-reading image area is water repellent while the nonimage area is receptive to water. Figure 1-4 illustrates the image and nonimage areas of the plate. The press requires two roller trains, a short one that coats the plate with a very thin layer of acidic water, and a second one, much the same as letterpress, to deliver a thin film of ink. When the dampening (water) system wets the plate, the water-repellent image sheds the moisture, thus remaining dry. The plate is then contacted with the inked rollers. Ink rollers transfer the ink to the dry images, while the wet nonimage areas repel the ink. This is the principle of lithography.

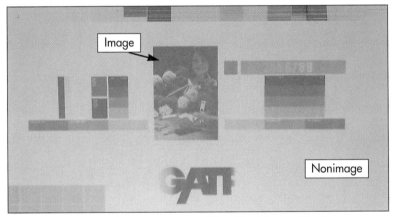

Figure 1-4. Image and nonimage areas of the offset lithographic plate.

The process is called *offset lithography* because it prints first onto a rubber surface called a *blanket* where the now-reverse-reading inked image remains wet long enough to transfer, offset, onto the substrate. It is really a misnomer to call the process "offset" printing since the offset principle is also often applied to letterpress and gravure. Figure 1-5 diagrams an offset lithographic print station.

Waterless lithography is another chemically based principle where the image area is ink receptive and the nonimage area is ink repellent. This is generally considered an improvement over conventional lithography since it eliminates the need for water and the entire dampening system. It employs a very-high-tack (sticky) ink

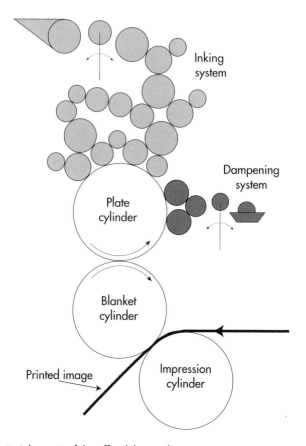

Figure 1-5. Schematic of the offset lithographic printing station.

that won't transfer to the nonimage area, which is silicone-coated. The print station is the same as in conventional lithography without a dampening system. It does, however, have to be temperature-controlled to maintain the tack of the inks.

Conventional lithographic plates are inexpensive in comparison to all other printing processes and thus affordable for even the shortest of production runs. The plates are exposed and processed on inexpensive machines, which further explains the popularity of this process for the general commercial industry that is dominated by small local entrepreneurships.

GRAVURE

Gravure printing employs a precision metal cylinder with image areas composed of tiny cells engraved or etched into the metal surface. This cylinder is simply rotated in a pan of ink, and its non-image surface is wiped (doctored) with a very thin metal, plastic, or other synthetic composition blade called a doctor blade. The doctor blade wipes the smooth surface clean of ink leaving the image areas (cells) filled with ink, which transfers when impressed against the substrate.

Figure 1-6 illustrates the gravure image carrier. There is only one moving part. Since it is a "direct" process, meaning the imaged plate prints directly to the substrate, it requires a smooth receiving surface that contacts all the cells or there will be voids in the image, sometimes described as snowflakes. Unfortunately, there is always a downside. The imaging process actually cuts the cells into the cylin-

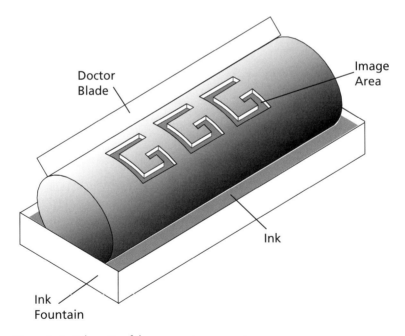

Figure 1-6. Schematic of the gravure image carrier.

der, usually copper. This means that to make a new "plate" requires cutting off the old image, replacing the metal surface, and re-imaging the new job. This is costly and time-consuming. If it were not for the cost of cylinders, this process would be a producer of far more than its current market share of approximately 11% of all print. The limitation of gravure to smooth substrates can be eliminated by printing onto an offset blanket which, in turn, can be impressed onto a wide assortment of surfaces. There are, of course, technical issues to contend with in all scenarios.

DIGITAL PRINTING

Digital printing, the youngest of all approaches, is most commonly an application of electrostatics whereby image and nonimage areas are separated by their electrical charge or polarity. The image is positively charged. It attracts negatively charged ink or pigment particles. These are transferred to substrates and fused for adhesion.

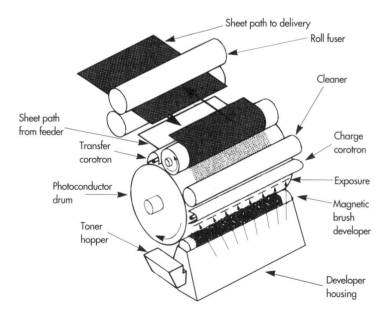

Figure 1-7. Schematic of the electrophotographic print unit.

Comparison chart of the major printing processes

Attributes	Rotary Letterpress	Offset	Gravure	Screen	Flexography	Digital
Ink Type	UV paste	Paste	Liquid	Viscous fluid	Liquid	Liquid or dry powder
Inking System	Roller train/complex	Roller train/complex	Very simple	Very simple	Anilox/simple	Simple
Image/Nonimage	Hard raised image	Flat/water repellent image	Recessed image	Porous/open image	Raised resilient image	No plate/image polarity
Repeat	Variable	Fixed	Variable	Variable	Variable	Fixed
Prep Costs	High	Low	Very high	Low to medium	High	Low
Image Transfer	Direct	Indirect/offset	Direct/can be offset	Direct	Direct	Direct and offset
Direct-to-Plate Option	No	Yes	Yes	Yes	Yes	NA
Substrate Versatility	Limited	Excellent	Limited unless offset	Excellent	Excellent	Limited

Courtesy J. Page Crouch, from *Flexography Primer*, GATFPress

Colorants may be liquid or powder, and image transfer may be direct to substrate or offset from an intermediate blanket. At the time of this writing, digital printing was in rapid development with new markets being seen continuously. Variable imaging of each impression permits personalization and a spectrum of new possibilities for creative solutions not available from traditional printing methods. A digital printing device is commonly installed in-line with other methods for its unique capabilities.

2 The Screen Printing Industry

Screen printing holds approximately 3% of the printing industry production by most industry surveys. The screen printing process is certainly accessible: shop sizes range from companies employing a single individual to larger print companies and suppliers employing thousands. The process lends itself to a diversity of applications as mentioned earlier. Many companies do not call themselves screen printers. They use the technology as a component in the manufacturing process. For instance the ceramic industry applies screen printing as a means of decoration. The automotive industry operates in a similar fashion. An interesting task is to identify printed products by the printing process used. Be prepared for some surprises and a potential obsession!

ORIGINS OF SCREEN PRINTING

The origins of screen printing stem from a device that is ancient in origin: the simple *stencil,* an impermeable sheet (such as an animal skin) with cutouts in the shapes to be reproduced. Held tightly against a substrate, and with paint, ink, or other colorant brushed thoroughly over the cutout area, the stencil transmits an ink image in the shape of the cutout. This simple device is called an *open stencil.*

Open stencils were used by the ancient Egyptians, Hebrews, and Chinese to decorate walls and fabrics. The big disadvantage of this type of stencil was trying to produce any shape that has a closed line, such as the letter "a." In these cases, the stencil loses the interior of the loop unless it is held in place by ties. The early Japanese eliminated the solid tie by holding loose parts in place with a mat of hair or silk glued across openings. The open-weave network formed a porous tie through which the colorant could pass. Stencil printing was popular in Japan until the early 19th century, and early forms of European stencil printing date to at least 1500 AD. The idea of starting with a porous sheet and then blocking out the parts not to print with an impermeable substance apparently did not occur to the ancients. Using woven silk as a screen in this way started experimentally after 1870 in Germany, France, and England. The process was therefore first called silk screen printing. Later, various other textiles (e.g., organdy, nylon, and polyester fabrics), meshes of metal (e.g., copper, brass, and stainless steel), and practically anything with a fine open mesh have been used as screens; therefore, the term "screen printing" has replaced "silk screen" as the name of the process. In 1907, Englishman Samuel Simon created a process of screen printing utilizing a cut stencil of the intended design mounted on a finely woven silk screen, a brush being used to force the ink through the screen in the cut-out areas of the stencil. Development of the process as a commercial craft first took place in the United States in the early part of the twentieth century. In 1914, American John Pilsworth devised a system for the silk-screening of banners, and until the late 1930s screen printing was used primarily for commercial purposes, eventually becoming favored among artists.

Through the years, a number of methods have been contrived for blocking out the areas not to print, leaving unblocked areas to form the image. The nonimage areas could be made nonporous by direct application of hide glue or water-soluble blockout, by a knife-cut stencil film adhered to the screen, and eventually by photochemical means.

An original, severe limitation of screen printing with respect to its development into a practical production process was the long drying time required by its inks, which were originally adapted from decorators' paints. Improved ink formulation and drying equipment reduced this time from hours to, in some cases, seconds. Such improvements enabled development of automatic screen printing presses.

Felt pennants were among the first objects to be printed by the screen printing process. Its use grew to the printing of banners, signs, and showcards. With the growth of chain stores and super-markets, point-of-purchase displays became an expanding area for screen printing use. Its capability for being printed on opaque or transparent substrates with a wide variety of shapes, sizes, and col-ors gives it great flexibility. Striking effects that can be produced by heavy or enamel inks and the way they can be enhanced (for exam-ple, by application of a velvet-like material called flock) provide special kinds of attraction. For these and other reasons, the screen printing process has become popular for poster, outdoor signs on metal, decals, polyethylene bottles, mirrors, T-shirts, circuit boards, greeting cards, and others.

DISTINGUISHING FEATURES OF SCREEN PRINTING

How does screen printing distinguish itself from the other printing processes? One point has already been mentioned—diversity. Flat surfaces and objects are printing problems successfully met by

screen printing technology daily. The ability of mesh to conform to surface characteristics is unchallenged by any other direct printing process. A second point is the various inks that may be applied to a substrate (e.g., paper, plastics, metals, and fabrics). The inks range from those used in typical graphic arts applications to conductive inks used in electronics. An added value is the variability of ink film thickness that may be applied. With screen printing, color gamuts may be noticeably increased, weatherability improved, and overall durability increased. Screen printer Michel Caza once stated, "with screen printing one can feel the image!" Variability of run lengths also makes screen printing a viable process for customizing products.

PRIMARY MARKET SEGMENTS

Screen printing may be easily classified by the wide range of market segments that it serves, including the following:
- Garments and textiles: T-shirts, coats, sheets, towels, and fabrics
- Home products: wall coverings, linoleum, simulated wood grains.
- Product marking: appliances, dashboards, in-line applications
- Large-format printing: billboards, displays, fleet marking
- Electronic printing: circuit boards, membrane switches, display coatings
- Coating market: UV applications
- Fine art printing: collectable prints, fine art reproductions
- Poster printing: low-volume displays

These market segments point once again to the diverse applications for graphic communication and manufacturing that screen printing affords.

TECHNICAL AND TRADE ASSOCIATIONS

As with all printing processes, screen printing is represented by local, regional, and international associations. Their primary function is to gather and distribute information related to the screen

printing process. The Screen Printing and Graphic Imaging Association International (SGIA) is perhaps the foremost technical association focused on screen printing and related digital applications.
SGIA's counterpart in Europe is FESPA. These organizations provide
industry and membership support via technical seminars, marketing
and sales workshops, and technical reports based on research. Additional support is provided to members through division meetings,
consulting, and information related to governmental regulation
education. Opportunity to network with industry colleagues is provided during the annual convention and internet connections.

Training programs are also available through supplier sources
with emphasis placed on specific product usage such as ink color
matching, color measurement or process control. Custom programs
of this type may be arranged on the company's site or through uni-
versity/industry consortiums. Trade publications carry calendar
events on a monthly basis and are a good source for technical information in articles. Investments in training for introducing new technologies in the workplace are rapidly paid back through increased
employee awareness and productivity.

SUMMARY

In screen printing, a stencil is adhered to an open-weave fabric with open areas allowing ink to pass. The stencil material prevents ink from passing in nonimage areas. Screen printing provides a flexible and diverse technology that distinguishes itself from other printing processes by adapting to many substrates and decorating or manufacturing applications. The individual components of the system should be studied and understood to make the best use of screen printing's attributes. With this point in mind, screen printing provides the client a unique system of graphic communication suited to many product specifications.

3 ARTWORK

The term *artwork* is a general term for text, photographs, drawings, paintings, and other materials prepared to illustrate printed matter. The artwork may consist of singular components or combinations of elements that convey the principal idea of the product: type, rules (lines), art (conventional or digital), halftones, or four-color halftones. Each component demands careful attention in print material selection in order to optimize the reproduction process. The printer should review the print job's artwork in relation to production system parameters. Careful consideration of both print and converting issues during artwork preparation will assist with the production workflow, leading to successful printing and finishing of a product.

This chapter provides an overview of artwork generation, assuming that the screen printing process has been selected as the printing method. The following workflow is suggested as a guide to understand the production workflow for artwork, assuming that digital techniques are used:

1. Client/designer initiates production of image(s) for printing; printer is selected.
2. Printer provides capabilities and services to client.
3. Artwork is produced: text, line art images, and continuous tone images are digitized for computer manipulation.
4. Initial digital proofs provide insight to job's status.
5. Files are gathered/composited and prepared for final film output.
6. Printing specifications are applied to the file(s) and final films are output.

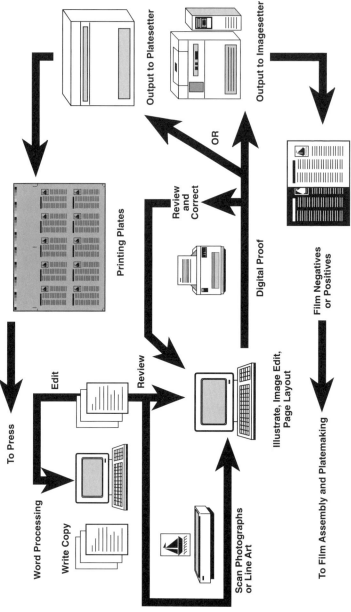

Figure 3-1. An example of the workflow in electronic publishing.

7. Final films are proofed for client approval.

8. Final films move into the production workflow.

GRAPHIC ELEMENTS

TYPE

Most designers will refer to the text in a design as type; letters of many styles may be selected for reproduction. Most type will fall into a classification system that defines the size of the type (points) as well as the face (the design of the particular type).

A complete font includes all the alphanumeric and punctuation necessary for a design. A font may include specialty characters such as ©, ¢, or ×. A complete set of one font in many sizes is referred to

ABCDEFGHIJKLMNOPQRSTUVWXYZ&
abcdefghijklmnopqrstuvwxyz1234567890$.,'-:;!?

Figure 3-2. A type font, in this case 10-point Chicago.

ABCDEFGHIJKLMNOPQRSTUVWXYZ
abcdefghijklmnopqrstuvwxyz 1234567890
Futura Regular

ABCDEFGHIJKLMNOPQRSTUVWXYZ
abcdefghijklmnopqrstuvwxyz 1234567890
Tekton Bold

ABCDEFGHIJKLMNOPQRSTUVWXYZ
abcdefghijklmnopqrstuvwxyz 1234567890
Helvetica Condensed

ABCDEFGHIJKLMNOPQRSTUVWXYZ
abcdefghijklmnopqrstuvwxyz 1234567890
Weiss Italic

ABCDEFGHIJKLMNOPQRSTUVWXYZ
abcdefghijklmnopqrstuvwxyz 1234567890
Eurostile Demi Oblique

Figure 3-3. Five different typefaces.

as a series. Further variations on the font may include bold, italic, and condensed or extended. Experienced designers will combine one or two fonts with size and weight of the type to convey a message. The graphic communications industry has its own system of measuring type, called the *point system*. The *point*, which in the U.S. has been set at 0.0138 in. (0.35 mm), is the smallest unit. The next unit used in this system is the *pica*. There are 12 points in 1 pica, and 6 picas measure approximately an inch. A printer's line gauge is used to measure type, usually in point units.

Screen printers should take note of the intricacy of the type. Fine lines or serifs on the type require better resolution properties of the printing system than will plain or sans serif type. Small type, less than perhaps six point, may prove difficult for a printer who has not optimized the print system.

If small amounts of type are used with a particular screen printing job, it is sometimes practical to produce the type by hand-lettering, photolettering, and using preprinted art type.

Hand-lettering is done by an artist who draws the characters with pen and ink or uses a stencil to outline the letter shapes and then fills them in with pen and ink. Hand-lettering is commonly used in screen printing if the stencil will be hand-cut rather than photographically prepared.

Photolettering is done by arranging film positives of individual letters of the alphabet on a camera's copyboard to form the intended

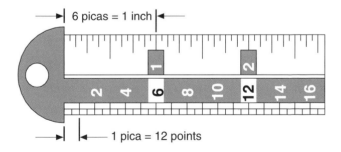

Figure 3-4. One style of line gauge, shown full size, with scale in picas and inches.

message. The arrangement is photographed, and the film positives can then be stored for future use. Film positives are available in a wide range of type designs.

Preprinted art type is a sheet containing a complete alphabet of capital and lowercase letters, figures, and punctuation marks for one typeface. Dry-transfer sheet and cutout acetate type are two kinds of preprinted art type and are good for setting a limited amount of display type. A dry-transfer sheet contains several duplicates of each letter of the alphabet. Each letter is placed in position and burnished onto the work. Cutout acetate type is an acetate sheet containing the alphabet and is backed with an adhesive. Letters are cut out and positioned onto the work.

Hand-lettering, photolettering, and preprinted art type are limited in usefulness because they are slow and tedious to implement. Today, the predominant method of preparing type is by using a desktop publishing system, which is briefly discussed later in the chapter.

LINES AND RULES

Line images are solid areas with no shadings or tones and include type, drawings, and diagrams. Line drawings are usually prepared with black ink on white paper or illustration board. If a line image is to be photographed, it must have high contrast between image and paper; black ink on white paper provides the best contrast.

Many designs will incorporate the use of a border or line to enhance an image. Lines are also critical to a membrane switch or circuit board manufacturer. The printed lines must conform to tolerance specifications, such as consistency, distortion, and amount deposited. For critical applications, screen printers should inspect printed lines by measuring them to ensure that no distortion is present.

GRAPHICS

Line work presented as an outline format is the most basic of graphic images. Many times the basic drawing gets added value by

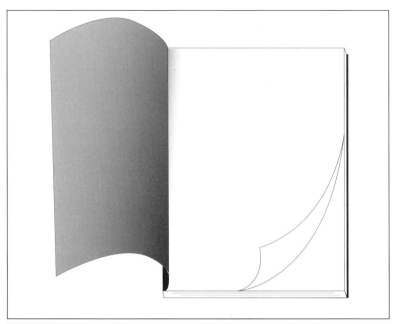

Figure 3-5. Two different types of images: line (top) and continuous tone (bottom).

printing additional colors in the line work. The illusion of many colors is produced by using tints of the color, meaning that dots or spots of differing sizes may be printed in the image to give the illusion of different colors.

Another type of graphic image is *continuous-tone copy*, which is an image with differing tonal values or shades. The most common example of continuous-tone copy is a black-and-white photograph. In screen printing, only uniform thicknesses of ink can pass through the screen to the image areas. Therefore, the continuous-tone copy must be converted into a halftone, either photographically with a graphic arts camera or electronically using a scanner. The halftoning process converts the continuous tones into tiny dots of varying size that produce the illusion of continuous tone due to the inability of the viewer to resolve or see the individual dots. When printed, the smaller dots will produce light shades of color, or *highlight* areas, and the larger dots will produce darker shades of color, or *shadow* areas.

Halftones are classified by the number of dots per inch or per centimeter. Several considerations are of primary importance to the screen printer required to produce halftones. The range of dots from smallest to largest refers to the tone reproduction range. The combination of mesh, stencil, and printing procedures dictate the printer's ability to accurately reproduce the original image. Another issue with halftone images for the screen printer is moiré, an undesirable interference pattern caused by overlaying two regular patterns. In screen printing, the regular pattern of the halftone images and the screen fabric's mesh may interact to produce a moiré pattern, which can be seen on a screen and is also likely to print. An optimized system will help predict and reduce the appearance of moiré in a printing job.

Reproducing a full-color image requires four specially prepared halftone images, each printed in a different color. The four colors of ink required are cyan, magenta, yellow, and black. The four halftones must be separated to very precise specifications. When properly manufactured, the four halftones can be printed in regis-

Figure 3-6. The same image made at two different halftone screen angles: 45° (left) and 90° (right).

ter to produce what appears to be a full-color reproduction of the original image. Printing four-color process images is a complex process that adds maximum value to a product.

THE DIGITAL PROCESS OF ARTWORK PRODUCTION

The oldest and simplest methods of creating artwork specifically for screen printing were to either hand-cut a stencil of the image to adhere it to the screen printing fabric or to paint the image directly on the screen fabric. The introduction of photosensitive emulsions for screen printing encouraged the use of film-based positive images. For many years film positives were produced on process cameras by photographing artboards that consisted of type and graphics that were manually assembled on a light table. Enlargements of images could also be made on these cameras, or negatives could be converted to positives in contact printing frames. Camera work reduced the need to manually produce screens for printing.

Then came the desktop computer.

In the mid 1980s graphic design was impacted by several production techniques made possible by digital technology. Designs could now be created directly on the computer. Workflow throughput was improved because of the computer's efficiency and accuracy. Never before had artwork and design control been integrated to such a degree. Artwork could be designed and multipurposed for a variety of print media.

The greatest impact was initially felt in the word-processing area. Drawing and page-layout software programs quickly evolved to meet the needs of designers. Adobe Illustrator® and Photoshop®, Aldus FreeHand®, and QuarkXPress® became the upper tier of design and output software used to generate images for printing. Design functions have now evolved to almost limitless possibilities.

In many cases, the conventional workflow has been replaced by a digital workflow consisting primarily of text and graphics generation and output. Overlay artboards have been replaced by digital files containing precise instructions for film output.

TEXT AND GRAPHICS GENERATION

In a digital production workflow, text may be imported as a text file from a word-processing program or input directly via a design or page-layout program. This production step will specify the type font, size(s), and styles selected for the job. Here the designer must be aware of fonts that are difficult to reproduce. The designer must also consider the availability of fonts downstream in production. Film output will require the fonts be resident when the completed file is processed.

Graphic elements such as lines and pictures may be input by several techniques. Artwork may be created in a design program with specified colors, scaling, and resolution requirements built into the file. Experienced artists and designers will build the job with production specifications supplied by the printer. Issues such as color matching, trapping, and fit (registration) are foremost in the design process along with meeting the client's goals. A second technique for acquiring artwork involves scanning existing artwork. Again, issues of color fidelity, size, and resolution must be determined prior to acquiring the image in order to satisfy print specifications downstream. A scanner may be preset for the specifications

Figure 3-7. Working with a file on screen can make a job move more smoothly through the creation process.

so the image is suited for applying final print requirements. Artwork for scanning may include line drawings, negatives, black-and-white photos, full-color photos and color transparencies (both negative and positive). Following image acquisition, further work may be performed concerning tone reproduction, gray balance, and color correction with very specific print requirements in mind.

Another alternative is to use preexisting digitized images. The majority of this work is found in image banks or CD-ROMs that may be purchased for use. The concerns to the printer in this technique involve image resolution and the permission agreement to use an image. Licensing agreements and written permission must be completed prior to including such an image in the final design.

OUTPUT

Final film output is an investment in materials and time for processing. Imagesetters expose the image to film by use of a laser. During this manufacturing process, all of the file's data is processed in the imagesetter computer. The file is translated via PostScript instructions, which the imaging engine will understand.

After the imagesetter exposes the film, the film is transported to an automatic film processor that develops the film. Periodically the imagesetter is linearized to ensure output precision and accuracy. To linearize the imagesetter, special calibration files are output. The films are measured for maximum and minimum densities, and discrete tint blocks are measured and compared to the calibration standard. If tolerances are not achieved, the output of the imagesetter is adjusted, and the new film output is again measured for the same quality control checks prior to proofing.

A wide variety of proofs are available. The proof serves as a reference guide for predicting print performance. A color proof provides a benchmark for color fidelity, register, fit, and image placement. The stencil imaging films are used to make the proof and contain all the print data, simulating production printing.

SUMMARY

Artwork has evolved from cutting stencils by hand from paper to highly complex digital files. Digital art usually holds to contemporary design principles, but all functions related to artwork production are completed on a computer.

Figure 3-8. Files can be output directly to a desktop printer or color proofing device.

4 COLOR REPRODUCTION

Color adds an exciting dimension to any graphic expression. The producer of the graphic attempts to bring the expectations of the customer to the finished product. Compromises must typically be made but careful consideration of the print objectives coupled with print realities can bring a successful completion to the color project.

The reproduction of color is both a simple and a complex process in printing. In simple terms color is a function of how much colorant is transferred from the printing plate to the substrate by the ink transfer mechanism. There are, however, many complex interactions which impact the color in the printed product. Understanding the color reproduction process requires study of numerous color characteristics and examining the interaction of process components. This chapter will discuss the fundamentals of color science, the color separation process, color characterization procedures, and current technology related to color reproduction consistency and accuracy.

COLOR REPRODUCTION

Color science may be expressed as the study of color phenomena benchmarked by human perception qualities. Through time scientists have tried to explain color by observing and quantifying experiments. A series of notable experiments were conducted by Sir Isaac Newton in the late 1600s. Newton studied the nature of light in order to determine its properties. He used prisms to direct the light and found light to be comprised of colors typically found in a rain-

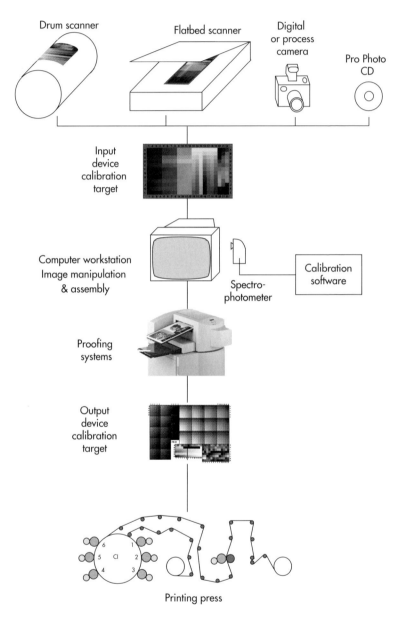

Figure 4-1. General concept of the color reproduction process.

bow: red, orange, yellow, green, blue, indigo, and violet added together form white light. Later experiments by others also determined other characteristics such as the directional properties of light. We realize light can be transmitted, reflected, absorbed, or refracted. Light properties are considered to be additive, which is one of the fundamental principles in color reproduction. A computer monitor is an example of additive color since the color is actually transmitted light.

Subtractive color theory refers to light reflected from a surface where the color of the light is affected by colorants that have been applied to the surface. The colorants used may be opaque or transparent. Colorants used in printing are called pigments; these pigments are a part of the ink that modifies the resulting color. Pigments are identified by measurement with a spectrophotometer producing a reflectance curve. Every pigment has its own specific curve shape much like a human fingerprint. Pigments are named and ordered in the Color Index, which is a reference used by many industries such as the textile and automotive industries. Since each pigment has its own color characteristics the printer must communicate the color requirements of a printing job. This is especially important in process color printing in order to obtain an acceptable match.

Before a discussion of color printing is begun several important points must be understood. First, three components must be present to initiate a color sensation: an object, an illuminant, and an observer. All three interact to produce the sensation of color. Any change in the status of one component will influence the color produced. The color discrimination abilities of the observer should be known. The type of illumination is also important since lighting conditions can shift the color.

A second item for consideration is color communication—the ability to accurately describe a color to another person. Color communication is also important as color information moves from one location or device to another. In order to properly communicate, a system describing color must be used. The simplest way to begin is to define the attributes of color—hue, saturation/chroma, and luminosity/lightness/brightness. Hue is often called the actual color such as red. Color order systems like the Munsell Color Order System typically name twenty or more hues including single colors (blue, green, red...) and combinations (yellow/red, purple/blue, etc.) The saturation of a color describes its purity or how "clean" the color is. The luminosity of a color is the amount of gray in the color from black to white. Notice we now have three attributes; this permits a specific point in a space to be located. With locations identified, colors can be ordered and differences between colors described.

A number of color notation systems have existed for years. Prominent among the ordered notation systems is the *Munsell Book of Color*®, which provides a numerical reference for any color in the *Book of Color.* Color science has provided support for color order systems particularly with numerical references supplied by measurement. In 1931 a group of color scientists met to discuss a set of color matching functions proposed by Wright and Guild. The Commission International L'Eclairage (today known as the CIE) began development of a number of numerical expressions used to describe a color. One of the color expressions most accessible to the printing industry is CIELAB.

The CIELAB color model is a three-dimensional space to describe a color. The L value describes grayness from black (0 value) to white (100 value) and is the center axis of the space. Colors are placed on opposing axes perpendicular to the L axis. Red (+a values) and green (–a values) are opposites as are yellow (+b values) and blue (–b values). Any color available in the color reproduction system may be accurately described by the three coordinates. Two colors (i.e., a target color and the reproduced color) may be compared with the equation:

$$[(L^*_1 - L^*_2) + (a^*_1 - a^*_2) + (b^*_1 - b^*_2)]^{1/2}$$

The result of this equation is an expression called ΔE (delta e). This value provides a means to communicate color tolerances.

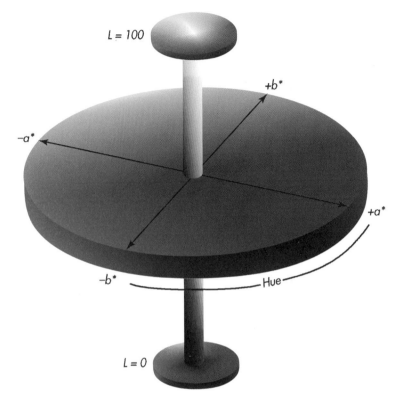

Figure 4-2. A graphical representation of the three-dimensional CIELAB space.

Many color measurement devices currently available will measure
and display a ΔE value.

SPOT COLOR

Spot colors are often used in screen printing. The ink colors are
typically opaque or semi-transparent. Colors can be formulated and
mixed according to ink formulas and may include mixing two or
more pigments to achieve a specified color. Ink manufacturers can
provide proprietary systems that cover a broad range of colors
known as a color gamut. Practically any ink system for screen printing can use this type of approach to print spot colors. The film posi-

tive records the image information to be used with a particular color. Textile and garment printers often use spot colors.

Caution should be exercised with respect to the illuminant previously mentioned. Under certain lighting conditions the spot color may appear to be a match; however when the illuminant is changed from fluorescent to sunlight the color may shift. Known as metamerism, this can provide unwelcome results. Ink manufacturers can help avoid metamerism problems when end-use requirements are communicated during the ink formulation stage.

PROCESS COLOR

The printed reproduction of color images with cyan, magenta, yellow, and black (CMYK) inks is termed process color. All printing processes use subtractive printing with CMYK inks; screen printing is

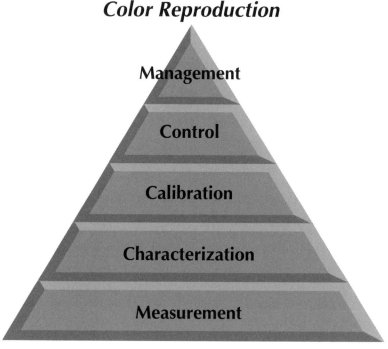

Figure 4-3. The hierarchy of tasks leading to optimal color reprduction.

no exception. The workflow leading to a process-color printed product is rather complex. The objective is to transform an image by a series of processes to create a set of separations which are representative of cyan, magenta, yellow, and black inks. When these inks are printed the resulting image is a reconstruction of the original image. The following sections will provide the details of the processes.

THE FUNCTION OF THE CMYK PRINTERS

Each process color (CMY) provides a record of a color image. Subtractive color theory describes each color subtracting one-third of the visible spectrum and reflecting two-thirds. Cyan ink subtracts the red light reflected from the white substrate and reflects blue and green. Magenta ink subtracts green light and reflects blue and red. Yellow ink subtracts blue light and reflects red and green. In short, cyan is minus red, magenta is minus green and yellow is minus blue. When the printer combines two of the process colors two-thirds of the light is subtracted with the results being the creation of blue, green, and red. As an example red is produced by printing magenta and yellow ink; magenta subtracts green, and yellow subtracts blue—red is the only color remaining. Unfortunately the three process colors printed together cannot produce a density required for shadow areas so black ink (K) is added as a fourth printing plate. Each color plate is a halftone comprised of small dots (highlights) which subtract very little light and progress to the shadow dots (largest printing dot) which subtract most of the light from the substrate.

REQUIREMENTS FOR COLOR SEPARATIONS

There are four requirements for a color separation that must each be addressed so the printed reproduction will print as specified: tone reproduction, gray balance, color correction, and detail enhancement. If any one of these requirements is neglected the printed results will be less than desired. Tone reproduction is concerned with the shape and contrast of the image detail. Testing the screen printing system will provide information concerning the range of tones

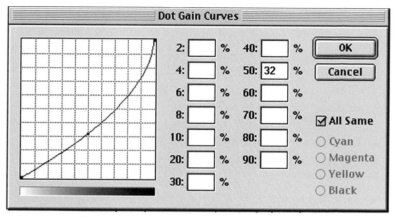

Figure 4-4. Applying tone curve compensation.

that can be produced by representative dot values. A more thorough description of the testing procedures will be described later.

Gray balance refers to the ability of the CMY inks to print in combination to produce neutral gray values. Due to the available process color inks not performing as theory states (each absorbing one third and reflecting two thirds) different percentages of CMY must be printed to achieve neutral grays. This problem with the inks is commonly referred to as hue error.

Color correction relates to the ability of the inks to reproduce "pure hues". Magenta has a large amount of hue error, as does cyan. Magenta acts as though it contains some properties of yellow ink, i.e., it absorbs some blue and reflects some green. If equal amounts of magenta and yellow were printed together to create red the results would shift more to orange. Therefore to achieve acceptable reds, less yellow ink is printed with the magenta ink. The inks' color properties are directly related to the pigments used in the ink set.

Detail enhancement can fall into a variety of electronic enhancements. The primary technique is unsharp masking. The term unsharp masking was used in photomechanical color separations to describe a fuzzy film image mask that sharpened edges within the image during the separation process. The sharpening effect provides contrast between image elements. In a manner of thinking the sharpening effect provides an outline between image elements of different tonal values. The sharpening places an "outline" within the elements. Detail enhancement is desirable in certain images which¡ contain jewelry, cut glass, or engraving. Caution should be taken not to overdo the enhancement.

THE COLOR SEPARATION PROCESS

Color images are "separated" by a scanner. The image is input through a system of filters (RGB) which defines the color intensity of the image and converts the light to digital data. The separator can then apply the necessary separation specifications through an image editing program. Photoshop® from Adobe® is the current defacto application for ensuring separation requirements are applied to the separated image. Highlight and shadow values are applied to ensure proper tone reproduction and gray balance. Color correction is applied via color lookup tables (LUTs) which are calibrated to the ink colors being used for printing.

Additional separation techniques include gray component replacement (GCR) and undercolor removal (UCR). In GCR, black replaces the "gray component" of the tone. (The gray component is

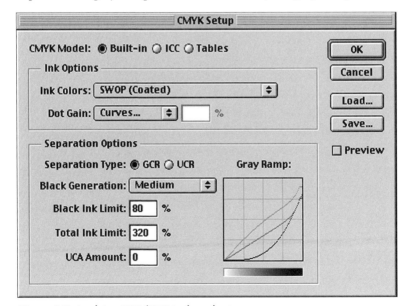

Figure 4-5. Applying GCR/UCR to the color image.

a neutral gray that results from printing all three process colors.) The smallest of the three colors, together with the corresponding amounts of the other two, are removed from the separations and replaced with black. The process of UCR is a special case of GCR applied only to neutral and near-neutral tones, unlike GCR which is applied wherever the three process inks are all present.

Both techniques provide advantages for printing. GCR enhances color stability and provides much improved setup during printing. UCR can offer better trapping and contrast in three-quartertone areas through the shadows.

DETERMINING THE PROCESS CHARACTERISTICS

Process characterization for process color printing requires planning, production, data analysis, and documentation. This is not an overwhelming task when each step is carefully addressed. The results can be an investment in future production capabilities. A model for optimizing color reproduction is as follows.

Planning process color print production requires communication among all production process areas: printer, separator, designer, client... anyone in the production loop. Keep in mind the major objective for a reproduction is to realize the client's expectations as expressed in the contract proof. Process characterization provides objective numerical data necessary for many stages of production, notably color separation, proofing, and printing. The purpose of characterization is to quantify the output parameters as referenced to in the original input parameters. Begin by ensuring that the screenmaking process is optimal for the emulsion, mesh, and exposure. The inks and substrate to be used should also be noted.

An initial test to be performed consists of producing a series of screen tints at selected line rulings, dot shapes, and screen angles. The test form should be checked for film density and the tint patches measured for accuracy. Following screenmaking, the form should be checked for proper exposure (remember to use an exposure guide) and moiré. The press should be prepared and the test form printed in a single ink color, preferably dark such as black. The results from this test will provide information on the tone ranges, screen rulings (counts/lpi), and appearance.

The color test should be planned based in part on decisions made from the results of the first test. Appropriate screen rulings and angles should be selected with the addition of color targets. The appropriate screen angles must be set at intervals of 30° for C, M, and K. The yellow must be set for a 15° interval. This will help minimize moiré between the color printers, but decisions should still be made regarding the halftone/mesh interaction. The color targets determine both the color reproduction characteristics and diagnostic elements. Tint scales in single color and overprints reveal tone reproduction properties. Gray balance charts combine various tint combinations of CMY to create neutrals. Solid overprints provide trapping information, rules of selected weights offer resolution, and type sizes in both positive and reverse establish reproduction benchmarks. Impression targets, register marks, and gradation scales

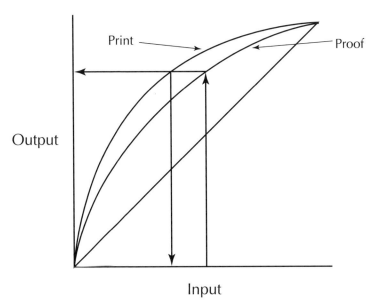

Figure 4-6. Matching the proof to the print.

should also be included. These targets must be placed on all sides of the test form so differences in setup can be recognized.

Complete documentation of the test must be completed, assuring accurate interpretation of data. Process teams should provide samples to the separator so that specifications for the separated images can be determined. One of the main items to consider is the amount of change from the input to the output. The separator can modify the images to provide optimum reproductions for the printing conditions.

The separator will typically calculate compensation for tonal value change (dot gain or loss). Tonal value increase (TVI) will produce a printed image that is too dark or saturated. The separator applies a compensation curve for the films. As each color is printed, the dots grow in a predictable manner to match the proof that was approved by the client. Other issues such as gray balance and color correction are also addressed.

While the technicians deal with preparing the films with the specifications necessary, the client will sign off on the color proof. The separator can calculate the output requirements to match the color of the proofed image(s) on press. The final print quality results depend on accurate transformation of the digital information to the press sheet.

COLOR MANAGEMENT

New digital technologies and tools have provided an opportunity to redirect color reproduction workflows. Previously the capture and processing of a digital image was destination specific. The conversion of the color images from RGB to CMYK were often made to default standards and print specifications were at times questionable. Specific software applications have provided a means to accurately define the color gamut of any device and transform the color data to a new device for "best fit" into the new device.

The working mechanism underlying the color management system (CMS) approach is the use of color profiles. The digital file format for using a CMS was developed by the International Color

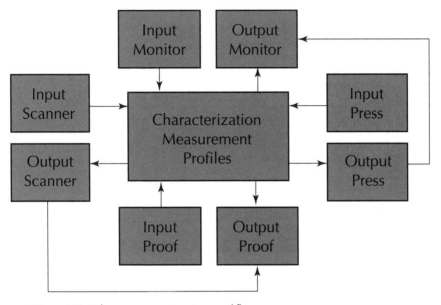

Figure 4-7. Color management system workflow.

Consortium (ICC). The use of a CMS brings device independence to color transforms. Spectral color measurements of the IT8.7/1 (transmissive) or 7/2 (reflective) scanner targets enable accurate color input. Spectral measurement of a printed color target such as the IT8.7/3 defines the color gamut of the output device. The color data are resident in the system as ColorSync® profiles for use with Mac OS®.

SUMMARY

Color reproduction requires careful and accurate color communication. Knowledge of color terminology and technical procedures must be completed to ensure success. Measurement and analysis of the printing system is required. The color image is processed with attention given to optimized input and the application of print specifications. The baseline for achieving success in color reproduction is meeting the client's expectations.

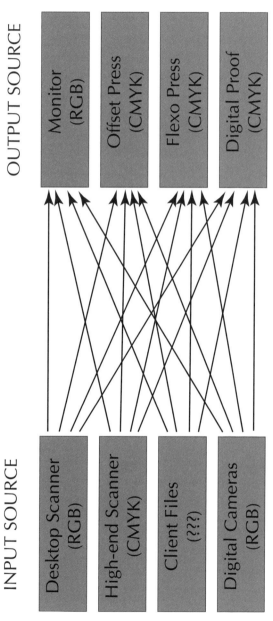

Conventional Workflow

INPUT SOURCE

OUTPUT SOURCE

Desktop Scanner (RGB)

High-end Scanner (CMYK)

Client Files (???)

Digital Cameras (RGB)

Monitor (RGB)

Offset Press (CMYK)

Flexo Press (CMYK)

Digital Proof (CMYK)

Courtesy Phil Green, from *Understanding Digital Color*, GATF*Press*

Managed Color Workflow

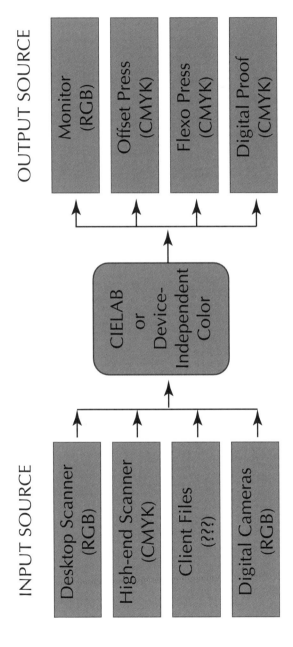

INPUT SOURCE

OUTPUT SOURCE

Desktop Scanner (RGB)

High-end Scanner (CMYK)

Client Files (???)

Digital Cameras (RGB)

CIELAB or Device-Independent Color

Monitor (RGB)

Offset Press (CMYK)

Flexo Press (CMYK)

Digital Proof (CMYK)

Courtesy Phil Green, from *Understanding Digital Color*, GATFPress

5 THE IMAGE CARRIER

An image carrier is a device on a printing press that carries an inked image either to an intermediate rubber blanket, as in offset lithography, or directly to the paper or other printing substrate, as in screen printing. The image carrier used in screen printing consists of several components: the frame, the woven screen printing fabric, and the stencil. Each of these components has its purpose in the printing process and may enhance or limit the print quality. In order to optimize printing, each component must be considered in combination with the other two components. This chapter will examine each of these image carrier components and end with the imaging process consisting of stencil application, exposure, and washout.

FRAMES

The four-sided screen printing frame provides support for the woven screen printing fabric; it must therefore be stable. Frames are made from various materials, such as wood and metal alloys. When selecting a screen printing frame, characteristics to consider include the following: frame size, durability, stability, cost, and stretching method.

FRAME MATERIALS

Until recent decades screen printing frames were made primarily from wood. It was easy to construct wooden frames of various sizes, and the frames were durable when coated with varnish or other sealant. The woven screen printing fabric was attached to the frame by several techniques: staples, groove and cord, or adhesive. The

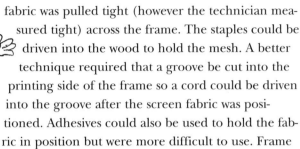

by Rafer Roberts

fabric was pulled tight (however the technician measured tight) across the frame. The staples could be
driven into the wood to hold the mesh. A better
technique required that a groove be cut into the
printing side of the frame so a cord could be driven
into the groove after the screen fabric was positioned. Adhesives could also be used to hold the fabric in position but were more difficult to use. Frame
stretching was definitely a nonscientific art in most cases. Tension
levels were low and were measured by dropping a coin on the mesh
and judging the amount of bounce. It was not unusual for the
frame tension to decrease considerably before printing began.
Careful handling of the screen fabric could permit restretching.

Wooden frames, however, had their advantages. The frames
could be easily sized to fit practically any job. Available woods
offered a cheap lightweight material that any framing shop could
supply. The frames were relatively durable when protected from
moisture by sealing.

Nevertheless certain disadvantages also existed. The wooden
frame is very susceptible to distortion particularly when higher tension levels were attempted during mesh stretching or during the
printing operation as the squeegee applies pressure. The image
could be distorted, leading to disastrous results in multicolor printing. Wood is a rather unstable material, and even if the frame has
been properly sealed, moisture will affect the dimensional characteristics of the frame. The least amount of warp in a frame will
cause the four sides to not lay flat on the printing table, again leading to distortion of the printed image. While use of a cord-and-
groove design permits restretching with relative ease, a warped
frame becomes a liability in quality printing.

Wooden frames offer a set of features that must be carefully considered during frame selection. Cost, size, and availability are points
that may be of primary concern to a printer, notably a novice printer seeking experience and low-cost access for screen printing. The
unstable nature of wood presents limitations in frame construction.

High-quality, high-resolution printing demands stable frames, which produce consistent, repeatable conditions. In short, wooden frames still offer a choice for frame construction, but with limited use.

METAL FRAMES

Metal frames provide a more durable, stable base for the screen fabric. Steel or metal alloys may be extruded in a variety of sizes and profiles for frame construction and offer the screen printer a virtually indestructible component. Metal frames are dimensionally stable and are also impervious to most screen printing solvents and cleaners. Newer metal alloys provide excellent stability with resistance to distortion under high-tension loads while retaining lighter weight even in larger frame sizes. Frames are available in standard sizes related to press specifications and may also be ordered for special applications.

Unlike wood frames, metal frames are not solid. Metal frames are assembled from extrusions. The wall thickness of the frame is designed to meet the desired strength requirements. The profile of the frame may also add further strength characteristics. The profile

Figure 5-1. A metal-framed screen.   Courtesy Intek

is seen in the cross section of the frame material. Common profiles are square or rectangular but additional profiles are available, depending on the frame size and press specifications.

The woven screen printing fabric is glued to a metal frame with adhesives. First the fabric is tensioned in a stretching device (generally a pneumatic clamp-based system). When the appropriate tension level is reached, the adhesive is applied and allowed to set. The complete cure of the adhesive may be instantaneous or require a curing period ranging from minutes to over an hour depending on the type of adhesive. Excess fabric is trimmed from the sides of the frame, and the frame is placed in the production frame inventory.

Metal frames offer an excellent mid-range cost alternative and are perhaps the most stable frame option available. Several further considerations are related to metal frames. First, the frame must have a clean surface to attach the mesh. This may mean extra effort when recycling a frame because mesh adhesive residue may have to be removed. Second, a tensioning system is required, which involves additional equipment purchases and an air supply in the case of pneumatic stretching systems. A third point of note is the preparation time required to clean the frame, stretch the fabric, apply the adhesive, and permit curing. In addition, a small amount of fabric may be lost due to clamping requirements in the stretching unit, although this amount is usually insignificant. Perhaps the major benefit of metal frames in combination with a stretching system is the opportunity to control tensioning and ensure that production requirements are met.

RETENSIONABLE FRAMES

The retensionable frame is another option available for screen printing frames. The retensionable frame technology was introduced and integrated into many production areas in the 1980s. The technology relies on the ability to move or rotate each of the four sides of the frame independently. The woven screen printing fabric is locked into each frame side prior to the tensioning procedure, and corners may be loosened (softened) to relieve stress and prevent tearing. As

Figure 5-2. Fab-Lok self-tensioning frames.   Courtesy A.W.T World Trade, Inc.

each side is positioned by rolling or moving the side out in sequence, the fabric is drawn tight. When final tension levels are reached the frame is ready to be placed in production inventory.

Retensionable frames are more expensive than either wooden or metal frames but they do offer advantages. First and perhaps foremost the frame can be tensioned rapidly, and tension levels can be adjusted at any time. During multicolor printing it is advised that screen-to-screen tensions vary no more than ±1 newton/centimeter, the unit of force in the metric system. This tolerance is easily achieved with retensionable frames. Preparing a frame for production is relatively fast as adhesives are not required. As with the other frame types, various sizes are available, and manufacturers can provide special orders when needed.

FRAME SIZE

Selection of the frame to be used must be made according to the image size to be printed. In general, for small frames less than 10 in. (254 mm) on a side, the frame should be 1.5 times the size of the image to be printed. This specification will allow free fabric and help prevent distortion of the image. For larger frames, this ratio is slightly less. For a frame with sides between 10 and 30 in. (762 mm) in length, the frame should be 1.4 times the image size. For frames larger than 30 in., the ratio is 1.35. Let's use an image size of 10×15 in. (254×381 mm) as an example. With an image of this size, the frame should be 1.4 times the image size. Therefore, a frame that is at least 14×21 in. would satisfy this requirement (10 × 1.4 = 14, and 15 × 1.5 = 21).

While tension levels are primarily affected by the mesh specifications, frame size as well as construction must also be considered. Higher tension levels place a great amount of stress on each of the frame sides. The frame may bow particularly in the center area of each side at high tension levels. The distortion will cause uneven tension levels across the surface of the screen printing fabric affecting print quality and possibly causing the fabric to fail prematurely. This effect may be minimal with certain frame constructions, but as frame sizes increase so does the possibility of the frame failing to maintain its squareness.

FRAME MAINTENANCE

Proper care of screen printing frames is critical. An unpredictable frame will probably produce unpredictable print. Several points should be followed in order to ensure frames will have long production life.

- Frames should be kept clean. All ink and solvent residue should be removed before and after printing.
- Each frame should be examined regularly for defects, failure/ wear, or nicks and burrs.
- An identification system should be used for locating frames in production inventory, stretching, or imaging.

- Frames should be stored in a cabinet, on shelves, or similar system and not stacked against a wall.

Screen printing frames are an integral component in the image carrier system. The frames are not indestructible. Proper care during use and regular maintenance must be observed to maintain high-quality production.

WOVEN SCREEN PRINTING FABRIC

The woven screen printing fabric serves two primary functions: the fabric supports the stencil system, and the fabric's mesh permits ink to flow through the image area. The mesh plays a dominant role in metering the amount of ink that will flow onto the substrate. The earliest fabrics used for screen printing included silk, hence the former name for the process: *silk screen printing*. Today, monofilament polyester is the most common screen fabric, followed by multifilament polyester, nylon, wire mesh, and silk, in that order. Nylon, for example, is often used for container printing where the fabric must

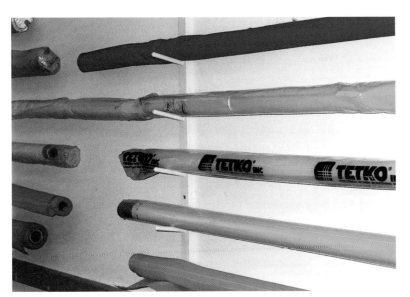

Figure 5-3. Different jobs may require different types of mesh.

conform to unusual surfaces during printing and then return to its original shape afterwards. Metallized polyester and stainless steel are commonly used when maximum stability is required and static is a by-product of the print action. The mesh may be grounded to relieve erratic print edges where the ink follows a conductive path onto the substrate.

This section examines the classification of screen printing fabrics, discusses the manufacturing process and mesh stretching procedures, explains how various characteristics associated with the fabric's mesh interact to regulate or meter the ink, and concludes with screen stretching and screen preparation.

by Rafer Roberts

FABRIC CLASSIFICATION

The screen printing fabric is a woven material. A loom (weaving machine) is prepared with the treads that will be fed into the the loom. The threads are of a specified diameter: small (S), medium (T), and heavy duty (HD). This is the first element of fabric classification and contributes to the durability of the fabric, tensioning limitations, and the thickness of the ink that may be transferred.

The actual weaving process defines another point of fabric classification—the type of weave. Perhaps the best printing option is plain weave fabric. Plain weave fabric alternates *the* weft thread passing over a single *warp* thread then under the next warp thread and continues the over/under process across the width of the fabric. The thread turns and the process is repeated but in an under/over fashion. A second weaving option is termed half twill, noted for a thread passing over one and under two threads. A full-twill mesh passes over two and under two threads. Both half- and full-twill weaving techniques are used to provide better strength characteristics in the mesh particularly when more threads per inch (tpi) are woven. Printers must be aware of the weave of the fabric used since ink patterns may be created by the fabric *footprint*, particularly in tint or dot areas.

A typical fabric classification system uses the number of threads per inch (mesh) measured in both the warp and weft directions. The fabric meshes are usually classified as coarse, medium, and fine. Coarse meshes run in mesh counts of 110 threads per inch (tpi) and finer up to 240 tpi. Medium mesh counts fall in the 305–355 tpi range. Fine meshes have a mesh count from 390–470 tpi and higher. The number of threads per inch is limited by weaving and thread composition technologies. The strength properties of the mesh can be lowered with higher mesh counts by the influence of the point at which the threads cross (called the *knuckle*). If too great a load is placed on the fabric, it will usually fail and tear.

A description of the fabric parameters can include the thread diameter and mesh count. Specifications include the term d, which is the thickness of a single thread, and D, which represents the total thickness of the woven mesh. The thickness of the fabric is measured to provide an indication of the volume of the ink that can be

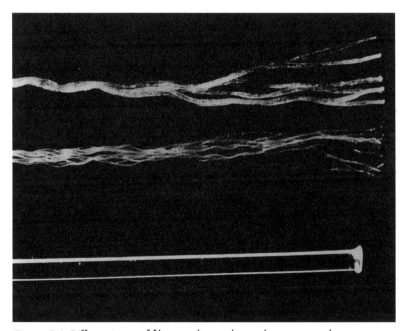

Figure 5-4. Different types of fiber can be used to make screen mesh.

held in the fabric for printing. The letters *M* and *O* represent the open area of the mesh and the percent ratio of mesh to open area, respectively. Again, the amount of ink that can be held in the mesh as well as resolution potential are indicated.

MATERIALS USED FOR SCREEN PRINTING FABRICS

The two basic categories of fabrics commonly used in screen printing are multifilament and monofilament.

Multifilament fabric is made up of many fine strands twisted together to form a single thread. The multifilament threads are woven together to form the screen mesh. Multifilament fabric is gauged by the *double-X system.* Used for many years for measuring silk bolt cloth, but not based on any real measurement, the double X is preceded by a number denoting mesh count. The higher the number the finer the mesh and the smaller the mesh openings. Multifilament fabrics commonly range from 6XX to 25XX. Most multifilament fabrics used for screen printing applications are either silk or polyester.

Silk, the original mesh fabric used in screen printing, is the strongest of all natural fibers. Each silk filament varies in width, causing irregular mesh apertures that can distort the printed image. Since silk is a multifilament mesh, it cannot be woven as fine as monofilaments. Therefore silk is only suitable for work where accurate registration and fine details are not required. Because silk has irregularities and a rough surface structure, ink particles tend to become lodged between the twisted strands, making silk difficult to clean. For these and other reasons, long-time users of silk have turned to multifilament polyester.

Multifilament polyester is less expensive than domestic and imported silk. It has more uniform mesh apertures and doesn't expand as much as silk during printing. As opposed to silk, polyester is not affected by strong chemicals used in cleaning or reclaiming the screen. The disadvantage of multifilament polyester is that the fibers tend to flatten considerably more than monofilament fibers at thread intersections. This results in a closing of mesh

Figure 5-5. Multifilament (top) and monofilament (bottom) mesh.

apertures that shows up in printing as saw-toothed image edges. Because of their construction, multifilament fabrics are thicker and have a rougher surface structure than monofilaments. They adhere well to knife-cut stencils and are best suited for printing where heavy ink deposits are required. Multifilament fabrics are usually used to print textiles, large posters, and textured or contoured surfaces.

Monofilament fabrics are constructed of single strands of synthetic fiber woven together to form a porous mesh material. Monofilament fabrics have a smooth surface structure that produces uniform mesh apertures. These fabrics include polyester, nylon, wire mesh, and metallized polyester. Monofilament fibers can be woven finer than multifilaments and still retain adequate open areas for easy ink passage. Unlike multifilament fibers, monofilament fibers are measured by actual mesh count per inch or centimeter. Therefore, a #200 nylon mesh would contain 200 threads in one linear inch (tpi). Monofilament fibers are available in a wide variety of mesh counts ranging from approximately 38 to 420 threads per inch. Multifilament fibers, on the other hand, can be woven only to 25XX or 30XX, which roughly corresponds to 200 tpi.

Nylon, which is available only as a monofilament, has similar construction characteristics to monofilament polyester with the exception of stability. Nylon is a very elastic fiber, making it a favorite for printing irregularly shaped or contoured surfaces. However, elasticity is an undesirable characteristic wherever critical registration is a necessity. Nylon is also affected by temperature and humidity, making multicolor registration very difficult at times.

Wire mesh, commonly called wire cloth, is commonly used with abrasive inks, such as those used to print on ceramics, or wherever extreme sharpness, close tolerance, and thick ink film deposits are required, as in printed circuit boards. Wire mesh is extremely stable and is available in very fine mesh counts up to approximately 635 tpi. Reclaiming these screens, the process of stripping the stencil from a screen so it can be reused, is comparatively easier than with nylon or polyester, and they can be reused many times. Wire mesh, however, has a total lack of memory, i.e., it will not spring back if dented or grooved, as will nylon, polyester, or silk.

Metallized mesh is a relatively new fabric developed for screen printing. It is composed of a monofilament synthetic fiber, either polyester or nylon, coated by an extremely thin layer of metal. In combining these elements, metallized polyester or nylon mesh has the advantages of both wire and monofilament synthetics. It will not dent or deform like wire nor does it repel indirect stencils without pretreatment as does polyester or nylon. The metal coating makes cleaning the screen easier than that of synthetic fibers. Metallized mesh has excellent dimensional stability and can be used for very long runs where close tolerances and exact register are a necessity.

SELECTING A SCREEN PRINTING FABRIC

Selecting a screen fabric is one of the most important decisions a screen printer must make. The type of material along with mesh count, substrate absorptivity and shape, nature of ink, type of stencil, squeegee composition and blade angle, the design characteristics, and the thickness of the printed ink deposit required are all factors considered prior to actual printing.

The following are general rules of thumb that can be used in deciding which screen fabric will best suit the printer's needs.

- Monofilaments are more abrasion resistant, available in finer mesh counts, and offer easier cleaning and ink passage than multifilaments. The screen surface must be mechanically and chemically pretreated to allow indirect stencils to adhere.
- Multifilaments have a thicker and rougher surface than monofilaments and offer excellent adherence for knife-cut stencils along with heavy deposits of ink.
- The open area of a mesh is the area between threads; it allows the passage of ink. The larger the percentage of open mesh area, the greater the amount of ink deposited during printing.

- Each mesh opening should be at least three times larger than the average grain size in the pigment of the ink, otherwise a screen will clog during printing.
- Mesh count varies according to thread diameter—the smaller the thread diameter, the finer the mesh.
- Thread diameter is one factor that determines the thickness of the printed ink film—the thinner the thread, the thinner the printed ink deposit; conversely, the thicker the thread, the thicker the ink deposit.
- The finer the detail in the design, the finer the mesh needed to reproduce it. For halftone and full-color printing, a mesh at least three times finer than the screen ruling of the halftone is needed.

Basic Steps in Screen Stretching

1. Inspect frame for any damage (nicks, old adhesive, etc.)

2. Select and inspect specified fabric. The fabric should be properly sized to fit stretching equipment and frame. Follow manufacturer's recommendations.

3. Be sure the fabric is square to the frame.

4. Lock or secure the fabric to the frame or clamping system. Loosen corners to avoid stress if possible.

5. Begin tensioning the fabric incrementally; do not exceed manufacturer's maximum tension specifications immediately. Experiment with rapid tensioning as well. Keep in mind the objective: a finished screen with the fabric at the recommended tension.

6. Measure the tension of the stretched screen and record the final tension level prior to placing the screen in inventory.

Fabric color is an important characteristic to consider, particularly as the color affects stencil exposure. Threads can be dyed to promote better stencil exposure factors; e.g., reducing light undercutting. Fabric colors available are typically red, yellow, and gold-orange. The fabric color filters incident light from emerging out of a thread and exposing the stencil in an image area, hardening the emulsion, and preventing printing ink from passing through to the substrate.

STRETCHING THE SCREEN PRINTING FABRIC

Stretching and attaching the mesh material to a wooden or metal frame is a major factor in preparing the image carrier. Overstretching or understretching the fabric directly influences the quality of the printed image. Smudging, poor registration, and premature stencil wear can all be attributed to incorrect screen tension.

In many small shops, screen material is stretched by hand. A device that resembles rubber-tipped pliers is used to stretch the fabric over a wooden frame. Tacks, staples, or the groove-and-cord method are commonly used to attach the fabric to the frame. Hand-stretching is very time-consuming and usually will not produce uniform stretching or the high tensions needed for synthetic fabrics on large frames.

Uniform stretching assures even screen tension, which is required for accurate printing production. This, plus the need for time-saving procedures, has led most large shops to use mechanized stretching devices.

Most machines used for stretching are either mechanically or pneumatically controlled. In either system, the procedure is basically the same. The screen fabric is cut slightly larger than the frame to allow a series of grippers or stretcher bars to suspend it above and outside the frame edges. The mesh is stretched to a specific tension percentage, which is dependent upon the type of fabric and mesh count.

A *tension meter* is a precision instrument used to measure the surface tension of the stretched screen fabric. Obtaining a specific ten-

Figure 5-6. Screens can be stretched manually...

sion level affects print sharpness, register, printing ink density, and stencil life. The tension meter consists of an indicator dial and a spring-loaded measuring bar supported by metal beams. When a

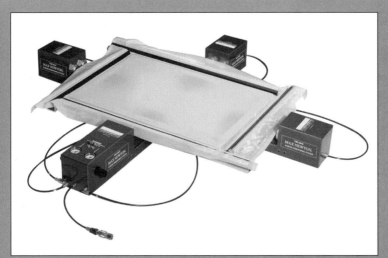

Courtesy M&R Sales and Service, Inc.

Courtesy Rhinotech

or mechanically.

tension meter is placed on the screen fabric, the tension meter's measuring bar pushes into the fabric. As the screen tension increases, so does the pressure on the measuring bar, and the tension is indicated on the dial. The tension variation *within a screen* should not vary by more than ±0.5 newton/centimeter (N/cm) for high-quality printing and ±1.0 N/cm for an average-quality job. The allowable variation between screens is just slightly higher: ±1.0 N/cm for exact register, and ±1.5 N/cm for average register.

Using a tension meter with a mechanized stretching device can make it possible to obtain the correct tension for screen printing and to duplicate tension accurately from screen to screen.

Figure 5-7. A tension meter is used to ensure proper screen tension.

In addition to separate machines and devices used to stretch the fabric off the frame, some frames have a built-in mechanical stretching system. Basically, these devices are composed of a hollow aluminum frame with adjustable gripper bars housed inside that hold the mesh securely. A series of tension bolts, which are accessible from the outside frame edge, are tightened, causing the gripper bars to pull the mesh in a straight outward direction.

SCREEN PREPARATION

After the fabric has been stretched and mounted to the frame, it must be properly prepared to receive the stencil. Generally synthetics tend to repel indirect stencils because of their smooth filament structure. For such stencils, the fabric must be lightly roughened to insure excellent adhesion. A fine abrasive powder is gently rubbed into the stencil side of a wet screen, then thoroughly rinsed.

Degreasing is the next step in screen preparation. *Degreasing* removes any grease or oil residue left in the screen from reclaiming chemicals. In the case of new screens, degreasing removes grit and hand perspiration deposited during the stretching procedure. Degreasing should be done to all screens, new and reclaimed, immediately prior to stencil application. This will ensure tight stencil adhesion and prevent stencil breakdown.

STENCILS

In screen printing, ink is spread across and passes through a porous screen fabric to produce the image. The *stencil* blocks the screen fabric to keep ink from reaching the substrate, thereby creating nonimage areas. The stencil should provide a *gasket seal* around the ink to prevent ink from flowing into the nonimage areas. Correct stencil selection depends upon many elements; e.g., the requirements of the print, the mesh specification, the type of ink system, and the length of the print run. Technology has certainly impacted stencil options in recent years.

The type of stencils used in screen printing can be divided into two broad categories: indirect stencils and direct stencils. An *indirect stencil* is first prepared mechanically or photographically and then adhered to the screen fabric. An example of an indirect stencil is a hand-cut (knife-cut) stencil, which is cut and then adhered to the fabric. With a *direct stencil,* the image is created directly on the screen itself. Although most direct stencils are created photographically or electronically, one simple example of a direct stencil would be an artist painting the image directly on the screen fabric. Several methods of creating stencils are discussed below.

Further, stencils can be subdivided into additional categories, depending on whether the stencils are created mechanically, photographically, or electronically. A hand-cut stencil for example is produced mechanically, using a knife. The majority of stencils currently are produced photographically; that is, a light-sensitive emulsion is exposed to a high-intensity light source rich in ultraviolet (UV) radiation.

Each system has attributes that may contribute to print performance and quality. Procedures required for correct use of each system differ: handling of the material, stencil application equipment, exposure equipment, and washout and drying equipment are specified for each system. Each stencil system provides its own print characteristics that must be considered: resolution, thickness, run length, and solvent resistance. Decisions to use a particular stencil system should follow a careful examination of the requirements and desired results for a screen-printed product.

HAND-CUT STENCILS

Early stencils were hand-cut from a material, typically paper, and adhered to the screen fabric by the adhesive forces of the ink. Today, most hand-cut stencils are created on a film base. In addition, a computer and a plotter equipped with a knife are often used to mechanically cut stencils. The hand-cut stencil is more commonly used by artists (serigraphers), school shops, and small commercial shops.

The working copy for a hand-cut stencil may come from a rough or comprehensive layout, or from a laser printout. Artwork for hand-cut stencils should normally consist of bold lines and solid areas. Simple or basic illustrations and large lettering are more common than sketchy lines and shaded areas, which are almost impossible to reproduce. Although intricate designs can be reproduced by hand-cut stencils, they are usually done through photographic methods because of the enormous amount of time spent in hand cutting. Hand-cut stencils are often used in the sign industry, where the lettering on the plastic signs, menu boards, and paper banners is large enough to be economically cut by hand.

The first hand-cut stencils were cut from paper and adhered to the underside of the screen. Today, most hand-cut stencils are made of film rather than paper. The two types of film used for these stencils are lacquer and water-soluble.

The stencil selection should be based on the ink used for printing. The ink and stencil must be of opposing solubility so that the stencil will not be dissolved by the ink. A lacquer stencil is needed if water-based ink will be used, and a water-soluble stencil is needed if the ink to be used does not contain water.

Both lacquer and water-soluble films are composed of two layers. The first layer, called the *backing* or *support*, is a sheet of transparent or translucent paper, vinyl, or polyester. This support is laminated to a layer of a water- or lacquer-soluble coating called the *emulsion*.

The film is placed over the copy, emulsion layer facing up, and the desired image to be reproduced is cut into the emulsion layer only. The cut emulsion is carefully peeled off, revealing the support layer. The remaining film is undisturbed and becomes the non-image area.

Lacquer and water-soluble films can be adhered to the screen with a traditional adhering technique. A damp screen adhering technique can be used for water-soluble films. In the traditional adhering technique, the film is attached to the stretched screen with adhering liquid. First, the film is placed under the screen, emulsion layer up. Then the adhering liquid (lacquer for a lacquer film or water for a water-soluble film) is applied to the inside of the screen to small areas and quickly blotted dry until the entire piece of film has been covered. The adhering liquid causes the film emulsion to become soft or gel-like, allowing the mesh to be pushed into it.

The damp screen adhering technique is useful for adhering large water-soluble stencils uniformly. With this technique, the screen is dampened evenly on both sides of the prepared fabric. The stencil is placed on the wet screen, and a wet sponge is used to ensure even contact with the fabric. Finally, the excessive water is blotted away.

After the stencil has been adhered to the screen, the area of fabric surrounding the adhered film is still open and must be blocked out or filled. This nonimage area is usually blocked out with a lacquer- or water-soluble screen filler. Some manufacturers suggest using screen fillers that are of opposing solubility to the film. For example, the nonimage area of a screen with a lacquer film stencil should be blocked out with a water-soluble filler, unless a water-based ink was used in the screen. If a lacquer-type filler were used it would partially dissolve the film. The support layer is then peeled off the emulsion, which has adhered to the screen. The removal of the support layer permits the image, which has been cut out of the emulsion, to pass ink from inside the screen to the substrate.

PHOTOSTENCILS

Photostencils have been the dominant process for stencil making in industry since the mid-1950s. All photostencils are composed of a light-sensitive coating or emulsion that hardens when exposed to an ultraviolet (UV) light source. To selectively control the hardening of the light-sensitive material, a positive is used. A positive contains opaque image areas on a translucent or transparent support layer. The positive may be either photographically or mechanically produced.

Imagesetters today can output positive film directly. However, if a process camera was used to photograph the original artwork, the resulting film negative must undergo another conversion process. One of the simplest ways to photographically convert a negative to a positive is through contact exposure. An unexposed piece of film is placed in a *contact frame* with the processed negative on top in direct contact. The films should be placed in such a manner as to produce an emulsion-side-up "right-reading" positive. The film is then exposed to white light and processed.

Some positives can be mechanically prepared. A knife-cut film with physical properties similar to lacquer-soluble stencil film can be cut and peeled in positive form. This knife-cut film, called *masking film*, consists of a translucent or transparent support layer coated with a red or amber emulsion that absorbs light rays of a specific wavelength. Open areas of the support layer expose the light-sensitive material. Masking film can be used directly with photostencil systems or placed in a process camera for reduction or enlargement.

The photostencil material is placed in contact with the positive and exposed. The image areas of the positive absorb light. The translucent or transparent nonimage areas allow the light to pass, hardening the emulsion. When the photostencil material is processed, the image areas, which were not hardened, are washed away *(developed)*, leaving the hardened nonimage to form the stencil.

There are four types of photostencil systems: indirect, direct, capillary, and direct/indirect. Each system has individual qualities that best suit a particular shop with particular job requirements.

INDIRECT PHOTOSTENCIL SYSTEMS

With an indirect photostencil system, the *indirect*, or *transfer*, film consists of a polyester or other plastic support coated with a light-sensitive emulsion. Some manufacturers offer two types of indirect film: *presensitized*, which is light-sensitive from the manufacturer; and *unsensitized*, which must be made light-sensitive immediately prior to use.

This indirect film is placed in contact with a positive and exposed to an ultraviolet radiation source. Processing indirect film includes a short bath in a developing solution prior to washing out the unexposed image areas. The emulsion side of the processed film is then transferred immediately to the underside of the printing screen, hence the term "transfer film." Adhering the film to the screen is accomplished by blotting the wet gel-like emulsion through the screen to remove excess moisture. The stencil, which remains on the underside of the screen, must be thoroughly dry before the support sheet can be peeled away. This support sheet, which held the emulsion during processing, also prevents the stencil from contracting during drying.

Because the indirect stencil is a very thin layer adhered to the underside of the screen, it comes in direct contact with the substrate during printing, giving very sharp print definition. However, it is this same property that makes indirect stencils very susceptible to mechanical damage. Durability is reduced since the material does not encapsulate the mesh. Stencil life is estimated to safely run between 2,000–4,000 impressions. Indirect photostencil material, which is a high-contrast film, is relatively quick and simple to prepare and produces very fine line detail.

DIRECT PHOTOSTENCIL SYSTEMS

With a direct photostencil system, a light-sensitive liquid emulsion is squeegeed into the screen fabric under subdued lighting conditions. Often, a coating trough or an automatic coater is used to apply the direct emulsion to the screen fabric. In coating the screen with a direct emulsion, it is important to fill the mesh openings and com-

Courtesy Liberty Screenprinting Machinery, Inc.

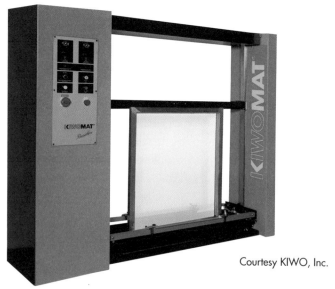

Courtesy KIWO, Inc.

Figure 5-8. Screens may be mechanically coated with a photosensitive emulsion. Some machines like the ones shown here can digitally control coating thickness and screen-to-screen emulsion consistency.

pletely coat and penetrate the screen fabric threads. Skill in coating is needed to produce uniform, pinhole-free stencils.

Several coats of emulsion can be used to build up the dried emulsion thickness, yielding sharper prints and thicker deposits of ink. It is important that the direct emulsion is dried thoroughly before exposure. A film positive is placed in direct contact with the screen and is exposed with a light source. The unexposed areas of the stencil are washed out in warm water and allowed to dry. Direct emulsions do not use a support sheet; therefore, stencil shrinking does occur during drying. Application of multiple coatings and drying between the coatings reduces shrinking. Two coatings of emulsion on the printing side and five coatings on the squeegee side are commonly recommended.

Direct emulsions contain water and a plastic-based resin (polyvinyl alcohol and polyvinyl chloride). The water keeps the solid material in dispersion until the emulsion is dried following application to the mesh. Most direct emulsions have a solids content of approximately 50%. This means the emulsion will shrink and follow the shape of the mesh threads when dry. The smoothness of the emulsion can be measured and has a ratio called *emulsion over mesh*. The numerical measurement is termed *Rz value*.

Although coating a direct emulsion requires a great deal of production time and skill, it can survive very long runs. Printing runs can easily exceed 100,000 because of the penetration of stencil into the mesh.

Direct emulsions are often considered to be the workhorse stencil material of the screen printing industry. Direct emulsions are the least costly stencil material, extremely durable, and versatile.

CAPILLARY SYSTEMS

The capillary system is a direct stencil that consists of a liquid emulsion on a film base. Capillary stencil systems have the advantages of being a faster method, less difficult, and less messy than liquid emulsions. The emulsion, which is coated on a support film, is placed in contact with the wet screen. Pressure should be applied by hand or by squeegee to embed the emulsion into the screen mesh. After the screen is dry, the support film can be removed. The screen can then be exposed with a light source, washed to remove unexposed areas, and dried.

The printing surface with this photostencil system is very smooth, and the consistency from stencil to stencil is easily repeatable. Print run lengths of up to 30,000 impressions can be expected. When a coating emulsion is used with the film, runs of up to 50,000 can be obtained.

DIRECT/INDIRECT PHOTOSTENCIL SYSTEMS

The direct/indirect photostencil system is a *combination* of an indirect film stencil and direct emulsion. A sensitized liquid emulsion coating is squeegeed through the screen to an unsensitized piece of film underneath. This film consists of a factory-coated emulsion on a polyester, paper, or vinyl support layer that is placed in contact with the stencil side of the mesh. The liquid coating laminates the film to the screen; sensitizing is simultaneous. After drying, the support layer is peeled off. The prepared screen is then exposed and processed in the same manner as a direct photostencil.

Some advantages of this are better control of stencil thickness due to factory film coating, a film support layer that helps prevent shrinkage during drying, and the combination of the very fine printing quality of the indirect system with the longevity of the direct system. Print runs range from 75,000 to 80,000.

STENCIL SYSTEM CHARACTERISTICS

The following should be considered when selecting a stencil system:
- Resolution and acutance properties
- Resistance to ink chemistries
- Exposure attributes
- Durability
- Ease in reclaiming
- Shelf life
- Resistance to water and other solvents
- Mesh compatibility

Each of these considerations ultimately has an impact on the quality of print and the cost of production. The selection of a stencil system must be based on the best opportunity to take advantage of as many positive characteristics as possible.

STENCIL EXPOSURE

An exposure test is recommended to optimize imaging and produce consistent results. Several steps should be followed to run the screen exposure test. First the exposure unit should be checked and cleaned. The stencil material is then applied to the mesh according to standard procedures. Next the exposure test guide can be attached to the screen emulsion. The test target should include lines of stepped weights, type, and stepped tints (1, 2, 3, 4, 5, 10... 90, 95, 100) of screen rulings you expect to use. Numerous targets

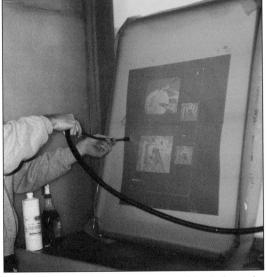

Figure 5-9. Once the screen is exposed (top), the undeveloped emulsion must be washed out (bottom).

The AdVantage® 150 metal halide screen expo-sure system.   Courtesy AmerGraph Corporation

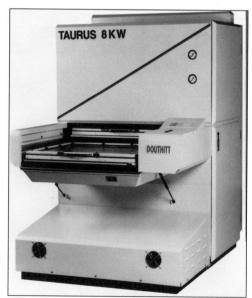

The Douthitt Taurus 8KW PCB exposure system.
Courtesy The Douthitt Corporation

are available from vendors, or targets can be obtained from film suppliers. The target should be exposed for a measured time, and the stencil processed according to normal procedures. If possible a number of exposures may be stepped across the emulsion by masking out the emulsion around the test target. Commercial targets have recommended procedures that should be followed for best results.

The developed stencil should be examined with a magnifier to verify the exposed stencil's characteristics. Pay particular attention to the color of the exposed stencil, the line resolution, and the tints that were not filled in or washed away. Once an optimum exposure time has been established, the exposure test should be repeated for verification. A transmis-

Courtesy KIWO, Inc.

Figure 5-10. Screens can be imaged directly from a digital file, similar to computer-to-plate technology for lithography.

sion grayscale should also be included to determine which step of the scale is held during the exposure. The scale can then be included in any future screen exposures to ensure consistency and repeatability. The target should also be printed to verify the exposure results and provide measurable printed data samples.

Although most stencils are exposed through a positive, a recent innovation in screen printing is the computer-to-screen imaging systems, which allows users to produce high-resolution screen stencils without film. One system uses a heated phase-change piezo inkjet printhead with a proprietary hot-melt wax to print a positive image directly to an emulsion-coated screen. The wax solidifies instantly upon contact with the screen and is totally opaque. According to the manufacturer, Lüscher AG Maschinenbau of Switzerland, no changes in fabric selection or emulsion-coating technique are required, and the imaged screen can be exposed with standard exposure systems.

SCREEN RECLAMATION

After the printing operation is complete, the screen can be stored away for future use (if the job will be reprinted) or reclaimed. *Screen reclamation* is the process of stripping the stencil from the screen so that a new stencil can be applied. By reusing the screen as many time as possible, screen making costs are reduced.

There are many methods for reclaiming screens depending on the type of screen fabric and the emulsions. Silk may be damaged during reclaiming, but nylon, polyester, and metal fabrics may be successfully reclaimed. Some fabrics are designed to be used for long runs and are meant to be stored rather than reclaimed. The instructions for reclaiming a screen are often found with the directions for processing a screen.

Generally screen reclamation involves cleaning the ink from the screen after printing. If the solvents used to remove the ink leave an oily residue, a degreasing agent can be used to make stencil removal easier. The stencil material, emulsion, films, or coatings are removed from the screen with the appropriate paste, liquid, or gel reclaiming material. For example, if the stencil is polymer-based, a substance such as sodium meta periodate might be used to remove the stencil. Once softened, the stencil's emulsion can be removed using high-pressure washout. After the stencil has been removed, a *ghost haze* might be visible. This haze may be due to residues of ink or stencil that remain in the screen fabric. A haze remover, a strong caustic solution, is used to remove the ghost haze

Depending on the size of the plant, screen reclamation can be done by hand, using reclaiming tanks, or with completely automatic machines. Hand reclamation is done in small shops where few screens are reclaimed. Reclaiming tanks are used when a shop reclaims many screens each day. The screens are soaked in the reclaiming tank for several minutes and are removed and rinsed with water. The use of reclaiming tanks removes the stencil material more quickly than by hand. With automatic machines, the screen is placed on a moving track, which carries it through the chemical solutions and the wash and out of the machine. This is the fastest method of screen reclamation and is used by the largest screen printing plants.

After reclamation a new stencil can be applied and the screen can be used for another job.

SUMMARY

The image carrier is comprised of several components: the frame, the fabric, and the stencil. Each component has its specific characteristics that can enhance the printing process. The components are also interrelated. Decisions on frame, fabric, and stencil selections may be determined to provide the optimum printing image for the screen printing process. Careful selection of the image carrier components will lead to better understanding of the numerous variables that impact the image carrier.

6 PRESSES AND DRYING EQUIPMENT

Printing equipment used for the screen printing process varies from a manual-feed and squeegee operation, called a *hand table,* to a fully automatic press with mechanical feed and delivery of the substrate. Three basic screen printing systems are commonly employed: the flatbed press, the cylinder press, and the rotary press. Most of the presses in any of the three systems can be custom-built or designed according to the printer's specific needs. Most screen printing systems use a squeegee to transfer ink onto the substrate. There is really no single type of press recognized as the most suitable piece of equipment for the diverse and versatile screen printing process.

The screen printing press is a machine with the capability to accurately transfer ink to a given substrate. Presses are a major investment and consist of many components, some common across all press designs and some engineered for specialized industrial printing.

Presses may be classified with reference to design, product, size, and image carrier type. This chapter provides an overview of press classifications to assist in understanding the role a press plays in production. Next, the common components of the press— squeegees, flood bars, registration systems, and feeding systems are described. The chapter concludes with a checklist for the press operator and a discussion of the main drying systems employed in screen printing.

BASIC PRESS CATEGORIES

THE FLATBED PRESS

Flatbed presses are primarily used for printing on flat substrates of various composition, size, and thickness. For example, flatbed presses can print on a wide range of substrate thicknesses, from very thin plastic and textiles to 1-in. (25.4-mm) board. Flatbed presses can be divided into three categories: hand-operated, semiautomatic, and fully automatic.

Hand-operated screen printing tables are still used in many commercial shops. The frame is placed in clamp-type hinges, which allow the operator to lift the screen between print strokes to remove and replace the substrate. Improvements to hand table operation have increased speed and quality. Vacuum tables or beds, which keep the substrate stationary during printing, improve print quality and multicolor registration. Counterweights and larger handles are attached to the squeegee to increase printing speed and to maintain a constant angle between the screen and squeegee.

Hand tables are often found alongside highly developed automated presses. They can be used for test runs of packages that will eventually be mass-produced either with automatic screen printing presses or an entirely different printing process.

Semiautomatic flatbed presses work on the same principle as hand tables except the hand operation of the squeegee and frame lift are mechanized. Vacuum beds are used to keep substrates in position during the printing operation. Feeding and delivery of the substrate can vary according to the manufacturer's design or the printer's needs. Some semiautomatic presses employ manual feed and delivery while others have manual feed but automatic delivery. Semiautomatic flatbed presses print the same substrates as the hand table; however, production and print quality improve because of the consistency maintained by mechanical squeegee stroke pressure and constant blade angle.

The automatic flatbed press and the automatic cylinder press are two types of presses used by most screen printers today. The automatic flatbed press is capable of printing on both flexible and rigid substrates—as thin as paper or as thick as 0.75-in. (18-mm) masonite.

During the printing cycle of an automatic flatbed press, the flat or sheet-like substrate is automatically fed and registered on a stationary vacuum flatbed. The screen is held in a carriage, which brings it into printing position above the sheet. Image transfer takes place as the mechanically controlled squeegee moves across the screen. After the impression is made, the carriage moves away from the bed and the squeegee returns to its starting position, coating the screen with a layer of ink called the *flood coat*. This is accomplished by a metal blade attached to the back of the squeegee that comes into screen contact after the impression stroke. The flood coat returns ink to the starting position but does not force ink through the image areas. This insures a proper ink supply to every part of the screen. Most automatic presses use the flood coating method. After the printed substrate is mechanically removed, the press repeats the printing cycle.

Flatbed press sizes vary enormously. Although the common press sizes range from 8.5×11 in. (215×279 mm) to 60×90 in. (1.5×2.3 m), presses especially for circuit printing are smaller than 8.5×11 in., and one standard flatbed press measures 78×156 in. (2×3.9 m). Speeds range from over 2,000 impressions per hour (iph) on smaller presses to over 1,000 iph on larger presses.

There are many variations of the flatbed principle, some of which are used in printing T-shirts, textiles, wallpaper, and electronic circuits. Flatbed web presses, for example, are used to produce labels and decals at relatively high speeds (150 ft./min.). Whether the press has manual feed and delivery or automated devices in any combination, the basic flatbed principle exists for all variations.

THE CYLINDER PRESS

The basic parts of the automatic *cylinder press* consist of a screen carriage, a squeegee, and an impression cylinder. During the printing cycle, the impression cylinder, carrying the substrate, and the screen carriage both move, but the squeegee remains stationary. The cylinder, which has grippers at the leading edge, clamp the substrate as it is fed in. The substrate is held firmly to the cylinder's surface by vacuum. As the cylinder and substrate turn toward the delivery end, the screen slides toward the feeding end of the press, causing the fixed squeegee to force ink through the image area. At the end of the print stroke, the substrate is removed and delivered, and the screen slides toward the rear of the press, ready to start the next cycle.

Cylinder presses with automatic feed and delivery systems allow speeds up to 4,000–6,000 iph. Sheet-type substrates such as paper, plastic, or flexible boards are commonly handled on this press, since most cylinder presses cannot handle rigid substrates.

Both fully automatic flatbed and cylinder presses are capable of printing at high speeds; however, cylinder presses are generally faster. Speeds also vary according to the type and size of machine and substrate. Generally, smaller presses can print at higher speeds than larger presses can.

The cylinder press principle is used in printing a wide variety of round, oval, or tapered substrates such as bottles, pails, dials, sports equipment, and toys. A stationary squeegee is mounted in a sliding screen, which moves simultaneously over the revolving substrate. The substrate takes the place of the impression cylinder. Presses that print irregularly shaped objects can be fully automatic, semi-automatic, or manually operated. Printing speed is affected by the size and shape of the substrate and the type of printing mechanism used.

There are few limitations in the screen printing of irregularly shaped objects. They range in size from 50-gallon drums to small lipstick containers. In some instances, flexible plastic bottles are inflated to give a stable printing surface. Substrates containing tapers, such as soft-drink bottles, are printed from screens with good elasticity and specially shaped squeegees that will conform to the surface.

THE ROTARY PRESS

Compared to the flatbed and cylinder designs, the *rotary screen press* is a relatively new screen printing system, with the first rotary screen printing machine introduced in Holland in 1963. A fine-wire cylindrical screen containing a squeegee-like blade inside rotates over a continuous roll of paper. The rotary screen mesh is coated with a photosensitive emulsion and exposed in contact with a positive. It is then processed similarly to most photostencil materials. The squeegee, which remains stationary, forces ink through the rotating screen as the web travels underneath. Ink is continuously pumped inside to maintain high printing speeds. The web, which varies from lightweight giftwraps and textiles to thin paperboard and wall-covering vinyls, is capable of traveling through several printing stations at speeds of 200 ft./min. (61 m/min.). Each station has its own screen unit that may be printing one of several colors or a clear final coating. At the end of the printing cycle, the web is transferred to slitting and sheeting units. The slitter first splits the web vertically, then the sheeter cuts the split web horizontally into sheets.

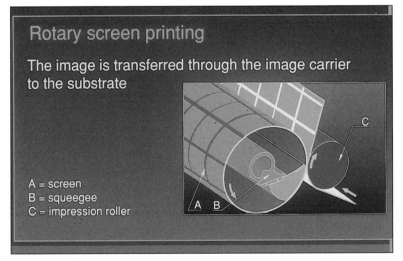

Rotary screen printing

The image is transferred through the image carrier to the substrate

A = screen
B = squeegee
C = impression roller

Figure 6-1. The rotary screen printing process.   Courtesy Stork Brabant, Inc.

PRESS COMPONENTS

Screen printing presses have many common features that are easy to identify. Screen printing presses have a device that secures the image carrier, an assembly for holding the squeegee and flood bar, a vacuum bed or jig to register the substrate, and various controls for adjustments (speed, off-contact, peel, and drives for more automated presses).

IMAGE CARRIER FRAME

The assembly for securing the image carrier should possess the following qualities: a clamping system to immobilize the frame holding the imaged screen mesh, control devices to adjust the off-contact distance, and controls for adjusting register (head-to-tail, side-to-side, and skew). In general, the clamping attachment should secure the frame at a minimum of four points. Ideally, this clamp is easily retrofitted to hold a variety of frame shapes and sizes. The assembly should be manufactured of cast or shaped metal design. The frame assembly can be hung from the press body by means of fine threaded screws and leveled with a level and a scaled wedge (for measuring the off-contact distance at the four corners). The register controls may be manual when screws are used or automatic when digitally controlled servo motors move the screen frame assembly. With this type of control the frame may be *zeroed,* and any subsequent frames to be used for multiple colors easily registered, reducing setup time. A last item to mention is the adjustment for peel. Peel refers to the action of the frame as it lifts behind the moving squeegee. This option is appropriate when printing graphics with solid areas and perhaps tints. With highly tensioned screens the peel action may be so subtle as to improve ink shear at the moment of ink transfer.

THE SQUEEGEE

The *squeegee* is a rubber or plastic blade, attached to a handle, used to force ink through the open areas of the stencil and mesh to the

substrate. The functions of the squeegee are to control the spread of ink across the screen during printing, to bring the ink-filled screen into contact with
the substrate, and—to a certain extent—to
determine the thickness of the printed ink film.

Ink is applied to one end of the screen. The
squeegee blade should be slightly larger than
the image area to ensure even ink coverage. The
width of the blade is a function of the image size. As
much distance as possible between the blade and

by Rafer Roberts

edges of the frame is recommended, but the squeegee needs to
exceed the width of the image area by a inch or two on each side of
the image width. The squeegee controls the spread of ink because
it is used to draw the ink across the screen, causing it to penetrate
the open area of the image carrier. This can be done either manually or by machine, depending upon the type of work, length or
run, or availability of equipment.

The second function of the squeegee is to bring the ink-filled
screen into contact with the substrate during off-contact printing.
Screen printing can be done either on-contact or off-contact with
the substrate. During off-contact printing, the screen is lowered to a
point slightly above the substrate. The squeegee is drawn across the
screen with downward pressure. Because of the elasticity of the
screen, the pressure of the squeegee forces the stencil into contact
with the substrate. As the squeegee passes, the stencil immediately
separates or snaps off from the wet print. *Off-contact printing* generally produces sharper prints by eliminating image spread and
smudging. The use of a vacuum base will prevent a flat, lightweight
substrate from sticking to the underside of the screen when it is
raised. In manual printing, off-contact can be established by taping
cardboard shims to the underside corners of the frame. Automated
screen printing presses employ adjustable devices that control the
amount of off-contact.

On-contact printing is done with the underside of the screen in
full contact with the substrate. On-contact is used when heavy ink

Figure 6-2. Sharpening a squeegee.

deposits are required. However, since image sharpness will decrease considerably, it is used only on substrates for which image sharpness is of little importance, e.g., textiles such as terry cloth or towels.

Squeegee blades are available in a variety of shapes. Different-shaped blades are used to print on different substrates. The simplest and most common profile used in screen printing is a square 90° angle. The general shapes and uses for each blade angle are found in the following table.

Squeegee blades are rated according to hardness, which is measured in values of *durometer*. Generally, soft, low-durometer, dull squeegees deposit more ink; while hard, high-durometer, sharp squeegees deposit less ink.

Squeegee blades are more commonly composed of synthetic materials rather than rubber, especially for printing runs over 200. Although rubber blades are easy to use, they tend to lose their shape and edge quickly. The introduction of plastic compounds, such as polyvinyl and polyurethane, has solved this problem. Syn-

Shapes of Squeegee Blades

A. Square edge — For printing on flat objects.

B. Square edge with rounded corners — For extra-heavy deposits. For printing light color on dark backgrounds or printing with fluorescent inks.

C. Single-sided bevel edge — For use mostly by glass or nameplate printers.

D. Double-sided bevel edge — For direct printing on uneven surfaces; bottles.

E. Rounded and F. Double bevel — For printing heavy deposits of ink on containers and ceramics. For printing textile designs.

G. Diamond — For container printing and applications.

Hardness Categories of Squeegee Blades

Extra soft	45–50 durometer
Soft	50–60 durometer
Medium	60–70 durometer
Hard	70–90 durometer

thetics tend to keep the desired edge throughout long print runs and will resist inks, solvents, and abrasion better than rubber.

Squeegee composition has evolved through the 1990s. Notable variations on the material used has resulted from manufacturers offering dual and triple durometer squeegees, fiberglass backing support, and the Combi™ which offers a more consistent printing edge. Dual durometer squeegees evolved as a reaction to the use of a metal backing blade. The backing blade was added to the squeegee holder assembly to provide rigidity—support for the squeegee to reduce flexing during the print stroke. One layer of the squeegee has the specified durometer for printing while the second has a higher durometer. Triple-durometer squeegees sandwich the higher durometer with two layers providing two printing edges: the blade is turned when the first side wears, offering more production time between sharpening.

The squeegee must be flexible, because there will be a measurable amount of bending in the squeegee as the force of the printing cycle occurs. Squeegees may be placed in the press at a predetermined angle. Nevertheless during the printing stroke both downward pressure and forward motion exert stress to the squeegee. If the material does not have sufficient resilience, the transferred ink may become distorted during printing. On the other hand the squeegee must be stable so a consistent printing edge will be presented stroke after stroke.

Squeegee profiles and durometer must be selected with respect to the material and image to be printed. A squeegee that is too soft or hard can distort the image or cause poor ink transfer. The following table provides guidelines to follow during squeegee selection.

Soft	textiles, garments, irregular shapes	low resolution, large ink deposit
Medium	most products	good resolution, varied ink deposit
Hard	flat surfaces	high-resolution graphics

FLOOD BAR

During the printing sequence the flood bar cycles to replenish ink in the mesh image areas. The flooding action of the cycle ensures that a continuous supply of ink is in place for the print stroke. Flooding also helps to prevent ink drying in the image areas when using conventional solvent inks. Flood bars are typically made of metal. Care should be taken to avoid nicking the flood bar, which can result in uneven ink flow and damage to the mesh.

OPERATION OF SQUEEGEE AND FLOOD BAR

The squeegee and flood bar are generally fitted in a holder and then clamped in the press (except in the case of manual printers who have a multitude of handle shapes to choose from). Presses will have a clamping system that fits the supplied squeegee holder or can be fitted to holders supplied by other manufacturers. Other considerations include adjustments for squeegee and flood bar angle. This ability can assist in improving ink transfer on inks with different viscosities or different squeegee blade profiles. The holders should have control screws for adjusting pressure—the best case is to have a pneumatic system to maintain consistent pressure during the print and flood strokes. During print setup the squeegee and flood bar pressures can be increased at staged intervals to optimize the best impression and flooding of ink.

The contribution of the squeegee and flood bar to the print is often overlooked or underestimated. Optimizing print perfor-

Figure 6-3. Installing the flood bar onto the press.

Figure 6-4. First the flood bar floods the screen with ink (top), then the print stroke (bottom) employs the squeegee to force ink through the screen mesh.

mance is simple: use three control points—speed, angle, and pressure. Whether the press is manual or automated these monitoring points must be addressed for properly controlled printing. Speed is

directly linked to the ink's thixotropic properties. The ink is formulated to move and shear when energy is applied by the squeegee.
Careful observation and measurement will help identify the speed
best suited for a particular operation. The angle of attack is critical
in transferring the ink from the mesh to the substrate. Practice has
shown that 70–75° is best for most applications. The flexing action
of the squeegee will place the printing edge at approximately 45°
with the edge at 90° to the substrate. A steeper angle may cause the
ink to snowplow, resulting in poor ink transfer. A shallower angle
will push the ink through the mesh, causing distortion in the
image. Pressure must be controlled to provide sufficient transfer of
the ink. To determine best pressure, begin with too little pressure
and increase in incremental adjustments. When optimum printing
is achieved, reduce pressure until the print breaks and then add
pressure until the print is optimal. The best pressure may be determined by examining microline targets, tint patches, slur or resolution targets on both sides of the substrate (flat), or similar targets
on containers. When targets cannot be placed on garments or similar products, pressure must be adjusted on setups and the targets
blocked out for production. The targets should be checked at regular intervals to establish printing consistency.

THE PRINTING SURFACE

The substrate will either lie on a flatbed, be pulled by a set of grippers at the head of a cylinder, or be secured in a jig for holding
containers. The printing surface includes both the impression
platen or cylinder and the substrate surface. In the case of platen
presses the surface must be kept free of pits or gouges. A vacuum
will hold the substrate during the print cycle. In the case of garment presses, an adhesive will hold the garment in place during the
print cycle. The images are registered screen to screen (color to
color) as opposed to single-color press-sheet-to-press-sheet techniques where three-point register is critical for substrate alignment.
Container presses may use an indexing system (that little notch in

the base of your container) particularly necessary for multiple-color register.

ADDITIONAL PRESS OPERATING CONCERNS

Quality issues indicate that press operation is not as simple as "set it up and print." All machines have some amount of inherent variability that should be measured and monitored to meet tolerances for the production requirements. A goal for press optimization is to know how a machine in question functions in normal production. In the case of plants with multiple presses, this data will assist in press scheduling. A side benefit is that the operator becomes much

---

PRINTING CHECKLIST

The following checklist describes the basic points of action and monitoring common to most presses:

☐ *Acquire screen from screen department.*
☐ *Check for improper screen specifications.*
☐ *Mount the screen.*
☐ *Make sure the screen is secure in press.*
☐ *Check feed of substrate. Consistency is key; check grippers/head stops, zero out.*
☐ *Register frame to substrate master.*
☐ *Put ink in screen. Check specifications for proper color.*
☐ *Place squeegee and flood bar in press.*
☐ *Coat squeegee edge with ink for lubrication.*
☐ *Set off-contact to predetermined points. This distance is affected by caliper of substrate.*
☐ *Make first impression.*
☐ *Check location and position of image. Adjust as required for impression/register.*
☐ *Measure ink deposit. Adjust if necessary.*
☐ *Obtain press OK.*
☐ *Run job—monitor consistency and quality.*
☐ *Clean and perform any required maintenance.*

Figure 6-5. The infeed (top) and outfeed (bottom) units of a sheetfed press.

more familiar with press variability and can more efficiently react to noted press conditions.

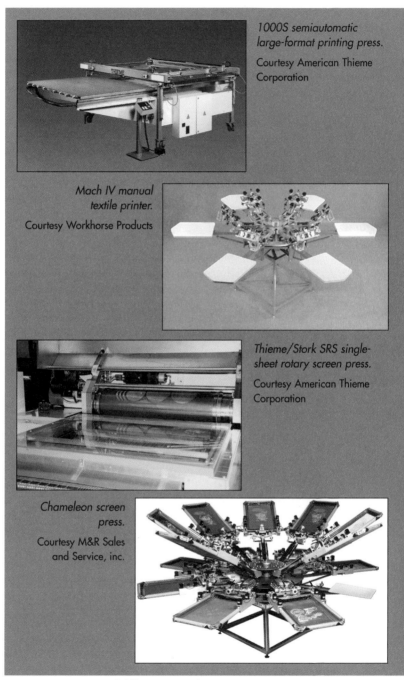

1000S semiautomatic large-format printing press.

Courtesy American Thieme Corporation

Mach IV manual textile printer.

Courtesy Workhorse Products

Thieme/Stork SRS single-sheet rotary screen press.

Courtesy American Thieme Corporation

Chameleon screen press.

Courtesy M&R Sales and Service, inc.

Figure 6-6. A variety of different types of screen printing press.

Hopkins 4/6 convertible press.

Courtesy Hopkins/BMW

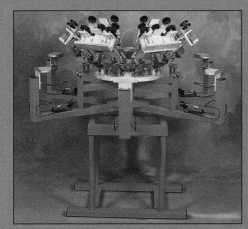

CAPS 6-color, 6-station cap printer with microregistration.

Courtesy CAPS Inc.

PT-8 Precision Turret Screen Printer

Courtesy Systematic Automation Inc.

A proper approach to meeting this goal is through measurements and procedures. The operator needs to have a tool kit of instruments for measurements used in data collection. The tool kit should include the following devices:

- Scaled wedge for measuring off-contact distance
- Tension meter
- Densitometer or means to monitor ink deposit
- Magnifier (12–60 power)
- Scales for making measurements

Procedures are foremost in any quality-oriented printing plant. Documented procedures tell any reader exactly how to do something, what to do, when to act, and suggested responses to various conditions. Procedures are easily developed by the practitioners on the floor—the operators. Direction provided by management will help during the documentation process. Procedures should be made available to all production personnel and updated at regular intervals. Any changes should be questioned as to the benefit or detrimental effects of the proposed change.

An accurate proof should be placed near the press. The proof reflects the printing expectations of all parties involved in the job and serves as the benchmark for print comparisons. Without a proper proof, the operator may use personal perceptions to determine how the print should look. This approach may not always sell the job to the client.

DRYING EQUIPMENT

The systems used to dry screen-printed products vary depending on the job and the size of the plant. The most common methods used for this purpose are drying racks, wicket dryers, jet dryers, infrared dryers, and ultraviolet dryers. Screen-printed substrates cannot be stacked or piled on top of each other immediately after printing because the ink film deposit is much heavier than in the other printing processes (lithography, gravure, letterpress, or flexography) and takes longer to dry.

The substrate and ink formulation determine the drying technique required. Generally, the manufacturer will print the drying requirements on the ink container. The screen printer must be aware of the drying requirements, which are a major part of each job. Drying equipment is available in various sizes and capacities or can be custom-built to the printer's specifications.

DRYING RACKS

Wood or metal *drying racks* are commonly used in small screen printing shops for air-drying prints. There are many styles of drying racks. Some consist of a series of shelves hinged on top of each other. As the substrates are printed, they are placed on a shelf, beginning at the bottom. Drying racks are usually equipped with wheels so they can be easily moved around the shop. In larger shops, metal racks can be rolled into a large oven that drys the freshly printed sheets quickly. It is important that air is able to circulate between the printed sheets. In some cases spontaneous combustion can occur if air does not circulate freely around the printed sheets.

WICKET DRYERS

Wicket dryers are composed of a series of lightweight metal racks mounted on a conveyor belt. The metal racks hold the printed substrate as it moves on the conveyor. Even with wicket dryers, air circulation is required to speed evaporative drying. Those wicket dryers without enclosed chambers typically have a fan attached. Wicket dryers that have enclosed chambers with forced air circulation and exhausting often have controlled heat as a standard feature. After the drying cycle is complete, the substrate is deposited on a receiving rack. Drying racks and wicket dryers are used for drying flat or sheet-type substrates.

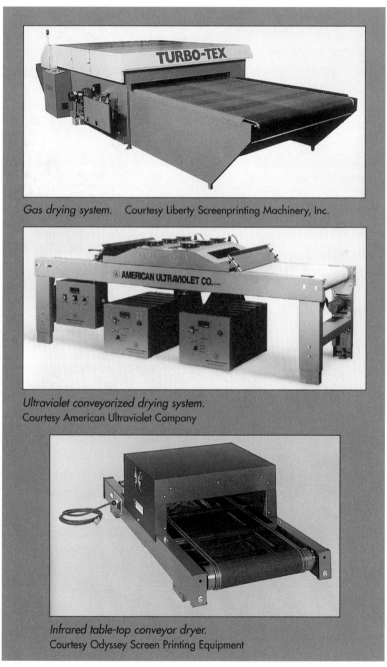

Gas drying system. Courtesy Liberty Screenprinting Machinery, Inc.

Ultraviolet conveyorized drying system.
Courtesy American Ultraviolet Company

Infrared table-top conveyor dryer.
Courtesy Odyssey Screen Printing Equipment

Figure 6-7. Three different types of drying equipment.

JET DRYERS

Jet dryers consist of a canvas or wire mesh conveyor belt that carries the freshly printed substrate through a drying section of high-velocity hot air. Optional cooling sections that circulate cool air over the heated substrates can be added. The cooling section quickly dissipates heat and promotes fast conditioning of the substrate for quick, efficient handling. Jet dryers operate on thermostatically controlled heat and variable speed control of the conveyor belt. These variables allow different adjustments for differing inks or coatings and substrates. Heat can be generated from oil, gas, or electricity.

INFRARED DRYERS

Infrared drying units use a conveyor system similar to jet dryers; however, the method of drying is heat radiation. A combination of infrared lamps and reflectors radiate uniform heat over the entire surface of the substrate. The amount of heat and its distribution can be controlled. The conveyor speed can be changed to match different inks, substrates, and production rates. Infrared drying systems are commonly used in printing circuits and textile printing, such as T-shirts and towels.

ULTRAVIOLET DRYERS

Ultraviolet curing units dry the substrate by a *curing* process. Curing is the conversion of the wet ink film to a solid, dry film. Curing occurs almost instantaneously, as the freshly printed substrate passes under a focused beam or reflective chamber of ultraviolet light. Conveyorized ultraviolet curing units can be designed to operate in conjunction with automatic presses and/or delivery units. These units can also be obtained to cure both flat and three-dimensional substrates. In comparison to conventional dryers, ultraviolet curing units are compact and efficient.

SUMMARY

Presses may be classified according to design, product, size, and image carrier type. Three basic screen printing systems are commonly employed: the flatbed press, cylinder press, and rotary press. In addition presses can be categorized based on their level of mechanical sophistication: manual, automatic, or semiautomatic.

Each of the basic screen printing systems have common components: the frame or other device to hold the image carrier, the squeegee, the flood bar, and the printing surface. The squeegee and flood bar provide a critical link in the printing process. Their cost may be insignificant considering the other print components. However, neglect in operation and maintenance results in poor print quality and loss of productivity.

The systems used to dry screen-printed products vary depending on the job and the size of the plant. The most common methods used for this purpose are drying racks, wicket dryers, jet dryers, infrared dryers, and ultraviolet dryers.

7   SUBSTRATES AND INKS

The material to be printed on is called the *substrate.* The substrate provides the printing surface, which will receive the ink. Screen printing permits printing on flat surfaces just as do the other printing processes. Screen printing also enables printers to print on irregular surfaces, containers, and, in fact, almost any surface that will accept ink. This chapter discusses some of the substrates most commonly used for screen printing applications, examines the properties of materials and how they affect screen printing, describes testing procedures that may reveal printability attributes, and discusses the inks that are used for screen printing.

TYPES OF SUBSTRATES

Most printers think in terms of paper or perhaps film when substrates are mentioned. Screen printing, however, can be done on a diverse range of substrates including paper and paperboard, wood, textiles, plastics, leather, metal, ceramics, and glass. Screen printing permits transfer of ink to most any material or surface as long as the ink will adhere and the screen can conform to the shape consistently without distortion.

PAPER AND PAPERBOARD

Paper and paperboard products that are screen-printed include greeting cards, posters, shopping bags, bumper stickers, decals, labels, and wallpaper.

A wide variety of papers and paperboards are used for screen printing. Among the considerations when selecting a paper for

Examples of substrates imaged by screen printing		
Paper	Plastics	Textiles
Paperboard	Polyethylene	Cotton
Steel	Polypropylene	Canvas
Aluminum	Polystyrene	Denim
Glass	Poly(vinyl chloride)	Wool
Ceramics	Nitrocellulose	Acrylic
Wood	Polyester (Mylar)	Nylon
Leather	Polyester	Masonite
Decorative laminates		

screen printing is whether it is coated or uncoated. Coated papers have a very smooth surface due to the manufacturing process, which effectively seals the paper. Inks, however, may adhere more readily to uncoated papers, but the resulting absorption into the paper can affect color strength and color uniformity. Two additional consideration when selecting paper is its *brightness* and *whiteness*. Brightness is the paper's ability to reflect light. Most higher-quality papers will reflect 80% or more of the light striking its surface. The whiteness of a paper describes how evenly the paper reflects all wavelengths of light (red, green, and blue) without a perceptible cast. Both of these properties affect the appearance of color reproduced on the substrate. Other paper properties to consider when selecting a paper for screen printing include strength, opacity, weight, grain direction, smoothness, and permanence. Paper suppliers can often provide sample paper specifications and printed samples to demonstrate printing effects.

Plastics

Plastic products that are screen-printed include containers, toys, signs, laminates, novelties, and panels for appliances. Some plastic objects, such as toys, containers, or novelties, are screen-printed on a flat, unformed plastic and then formed into the final product. Polycarbonates, polyvinyl, polyester, and polystyrene are just a few of the plastics that may be screen-printed.

The surface of plastics is usually smooth and glossy or textured as a matte finish. A property of plastics that may impact the printability of the material is surface tension. Surface tension is measured in dynes. Basically, if the surface energy of the plastic is too high, the ink will not adhere and may be repelled. A process called *corona treatment* reduces surface tension in order to enhance ink adhesion. The treatment is not permanent but does give the printer a window of opportunity for printing. Plastic materials such as polypropylene and polyethylene require corona treating.

WOOD

Wood products that are screen-printed include signs, paneling, and clock faces. Consideration must be given to inks that are used to print wooden signs that must withstand weathering. Some manufacturing processes may use a transfer or decal process to create the image that is then applied to the wood.

METALS

Metal products that are screen-printed include pails, barrels, 50-gallon drums, outdoor metal signs, identification plates, and pots and pans. Metals that can be screen-printed include steel, aluminum, copper, bronze, and iron, among others. A primary characteristic of a metal substrate is the stability that exceeds most other types of materials.

Some manufacturing processes may use a transfer or decal process to create the image that is then applied to the metal.

TEXTILES

Printing on rolls of cloth or finished garments is a large segment of the screen printing industry. Textile products that are screen printed include bolts of fabric, bedsheets, towels, and manufactured garments (clothing) such as T-shirts, caps, sweatshirts, and jackets. A garment is usually completely manufactured before it is screen -printed.

Examples of products produced by screen printing

Posters and displays	Printed circuits	Awnings
Greeting cards	Plastic bottles	Calendars
T-shirts	Glass bottles	Wallpaper
Highway signs	Food packages	Shower curtains
Nameplates	Perfume bottles	Floor covering
Clock faces	Fine art serigraphs	Apparel

Rotary screen printing is used to print graphics on continuous rolls of cloth to be converted into such products as sheets. Specially formulated inks often including dyes are used in presses of up to sixteen units. A variety of screen printing presses are used to screen-print garments, including oval printers and carrousel printers.

Of particular importance to garment printers is the weave of the material, the color (white, light, or dark), and the material composition (cotton, polyester blends, etc.).

The two ways to apply color to textiles are with dyes and inks. Dyes penetrate the fabric, giving it a new permanent color that can withstand washing, ironing, wear, and perspiration. When dyes are used, the design can be seen on the reverse side of the fabric. Inks do not penetrate the fabric as completely as dyes. A printed design coats the surface of the fabric and is not seen as clearly on the reverse side as are dyes. The decision of whether to use a dye or a printing ink depends on the fabric and the end-use of the printed product.

GLASS AND CERAMICS

Ceramic and glass products that are screen-printed include cups and dishes, drinking glasses, jewelry, mirrors, cosmetic containers, and vases.

Screen printing on ceramics and glass is handled in two different ways. One method is to print directly on the product. The other method is to print on a decal or transfer and then adhere it to the ceramic or glass product. Decals may use inks that become permanent following a curing procedure involving high heat in a controlled environment (such as a kiln).

SUBSTRATE PERFORMANCE

The substrate printed on has characteristics that influence the lay-down of the ink. Screen printers should understand what measures of performance can affect the appearance of the product. A listing of important measures follows.

ADHESION

Ink has to adhere to the substrate; this measure can be determined by a tape test. Tape is applied to the ink surface. Following a length of time (approximately thirty seconds), the tape is pulled from the substrate. The product is examined to see how much ink remains. Plastics may be checked for adhesion in a similar manner. Prior to applying the tape the ink is scribed with a sharp blade in a cross-hatch pattern. When the tape is pulled, the product is again examined to look at how much ink was pulled from the substrate.

DIMENSIONAL STABILITY

The substrate should retain its original shape after being printed. The material may distort during heat curing, producing register problems during subsequent printing and finishing operations. Stability is influenced by grain direction (papers) and elastic memory (plastics).

WEATHERABILITY

The printed product or a prototype can be exposed to water to determine its ability to withstand intended environmental conditions.

LIGHTFASTNESS/BLEEDING/TINTING

The material and ink are examined to detect fading due to light (particularly ultraviolet), and the ink's interaction with the substrate.

OPACITY

The material's ability to prevent light from transmitting or passing through.

SCREEN PRINTING INKS

Screen printing inks are often referred to as "paints" (especially by sign makers and display printers) because of their similarity to some sign paints and because they are often applied at thicknesses far greater than most printing inks. However, their formulations indicate that they are correctly called "inks."

Because of the diversity of products, the volume for any one screen printing ink is limited. Even more than inks for sheetfed lithography, screen printing inks are specially formulated for a particular job. Inks may even be formulated differently to print the same job on different presses: a fast press requires a somewhat different ink than a slower press.

Screen printing applies the thickest film of any common printing process, making it excellent for fluorescent and light-resistant inks. The thick film applied by a screen is often one of its advantages, but as a result of technology, screen printing can also apply a thin film— one as thin as or thinner than the film applied by rotogravure.

Screen printing inks differ from other printing inks in another important way. To transfer well from roller to roller, most printing inks must be "long," i.e., they must show some tendency to form a string when pulled away from a wet surface. Screen printing inks do not have to transfer from one roller to another. Therefore, they are short and "buttery." Short inks pass through the openings of the screen without leaving fuzzy edges. If the inks were long, they would form strings when the screen was lifted from the wet print; these strings would ruin the print.

Most screen printing inks dry by evaporation: high-velocity, hot-air dryers, wicket dryers, simple drying racks, flame dryers, and even microwave dryers are used. Ultraviolet (UV) drying systems solve one of the screen printer's greatest problems: slow ink drying. Continuing development of UV-curing technology has led to the manufacture of a broad range of UV-curable inks for a variety of applications. UV inks are used regularly to print plastic bottles, containers, point-of-purchase displays, pressure-sensitive decals, printed circuits for the electronics industry, and membrane switches for the automotive industry.

COMPONENTS OF INKS AND INK SYSTEMS

The principle components of a printing ink are pigments or dyes (colorants), vehicles, and additives. An ink can be opaque or transparent, depending on the ink's components.

COLORANTS

All printing inks consist of a colorant, almost always a pigment but occasionally a dye. Dyes are soluble in a solvent or vehicle, while pigments are insoluble.

Pigments are finely ground solid materials that impart colors to inks. The nature and amount of pigment that an ink contains, as well as the type of vehicle, contribute to the ink's body and working properties.

Pigments can be organic or inorganic. Organic pigments tend to produce transparent inks, which are used for process-color printing, while inorganic pigments tend to produce opaque inks.

The term *organic* means "derived from living organisms." Organic pigments are made from petroleum products: blacks by burning gas or oil, other colors be reacting organic chemicals derived from petroleum. The most common black pigment, furnace black, is made by burning atomized mineral oil in brick-lined furnaces with a carefully controlled supply of air. The products of combustion are cooled, and the pigment is collected with electronic precipitators or in bag filters.

Inorganic pigments are formed by precipitation—that is, by mixing chemicals that react to form the insoluble pigment, which then precipitates, or settles out. The most common white inorganic pigment is titanium dioxide. Inks made from titanium oxide are very opaque and have excellent colorfastness.

VEHICLES

The vehicle carries the pigment and adheres it to the substrate. In addition, it gives an ink its consistency. The vehicle is composed mostly of a varnish, which is a solvent plus resin and/or drying oil, along with waxes, driers, and other additives. The vehicle carries the pigment, controls the flow of the ink or varnish on the press, and, after drying, binds the pigment to the substrate. Vehicles also control the film properties of dried ink, such as gloss and rub resistance. The resins are formulated to optimize the ink's ability to adhere to a substrate.

The solvent serves to maintain the vehicle's flow until curing. The solvent is carefully selected for its compatibility with the vehicle and the substrate. Different ink systems use specific solvents to enable the ink to function properly.

The solvent in the ink can flash off during curing. The solvent products are termed volatile organic compounds (VOCs) and are regulated by government agencies. Most ink systems producing VOCs contain petroleum-derived solvents. Consult the Material Safety Data Sheets (MSDS) for the content of the ink system. Note handling and disposal instructions as well.

ADDITIVES

Most ink systems offer greater versatility through additives, which change an ink's out-of-the-can personality. Toners will provide greater color strength while mixing, and halftone bases reduce color strength. Thinners will change viscosity, and adhesion promoters improve adhesion. The printer must consult with the ink supplier concerning the use of additives. Improper use typically results in poor ink performance.

SCREEN PRINTING INKS FOR SPECIFIC APPLICATIONS

DECALCOMANIAS

Pressure-sensitive decals or waterslide decal transfers are usually printed by screen because the process delivers thick, opaque films with enough flexibility to withstand the movement of the carrier paper while they are being transferred. These inks usually require good light resistance. UV inks have been used to successfully screen-print pressure-sensitive decals.

CIRCUIT BOARDS

When a thick film is required on a printed circuit, the screen printing process is often the best way to print it. The ink must adhere to clean copper and resist the chemicals used in etching the copper to produce the circuit. If it is necessary that the ink be removed with a solvent or alkali after etching, the ink must be sensitive to solvent or alkali.

POSTERS

Posters are printed with poster inks on a variety of board and paper stocks. Nonoxidizing resins and oxidative drying inks are used the most. Overprinting with a gloss varnish extends the life of the print.

METALS

Enamel inks formulated from oil-based alkyds modified with melamine or urea formaldehyde, cellulose lacquer, epoxies, and other synthetic resins yield attractive signs for outdoor use.

The metal surface must be thoroughly degreased; aluminum is often anodized or given a nitrocellulose wash for the ink to adhere well. Baking enamels yields a product that is tough and has good resistance to aging, light, and weather.

Even more permanent are vitreous-enameled aluminum and steel products. Vitreous enamels are glasslike material or frit ground

Screen Printing Inks for Special Applications

Poster inks	Used for general graphics printing
Plastisol inks	Primarily used in garment printing (t-shirts). May include additives which puff when ink is cured
Textile inks	Also used in garment printing and on large textile presses
Decal inks	Suited for labeling and long lasting/weatherability properties
Pastes	Found in industrial electronics printing
Ceramic inks	Inks may be printed on decals then transferred to product for firing. Ceramic inks are permanent
Epoxy inks	A two-part ink cures by oxidation with the hardener. Excellent durability
Vinyl inks	Formulated to work with vinyl. Surface tension issues and off-gassing of the vinyl are primary concerns.
Speciality inks	Inks may be specially formulated to print with a particular material such as polycarbonates, polyethylene, or other types of plastics.

together with oxide colorants, clay, and water. After degreasing and surface treatment of the aluminum, it may be screen-printed with enamel based on borosilicates and immediately fired (without drying) at very high temperatures.

PLASTICS

Pigments for plastic printing must not migrate or bleed into the plastic. The solvent must be able to etch the plastic enough to improve adhesion without causing crazing (stress cracking of the plastic surface). Thermoplastic adhesives or binders are helpful if the plastic is to be vacuum-formed after printing.

The awkward shapes of polyethylene bottles are readily screen-printed, and the thick ink deposits provide glossy and bright colors.

GLASS

Inks for glass are either enamels or frits that are fired at high temperatures, or epoxy or other plastics that are baked at lower temperatures. Oil-based and synthetic resin-solvent-based inks are used to print items like dials, mirrors, and glass signs. UV inks are used to decorate mirrors.

Special inks may be used for windshield applications in the automotive and aviation industries. Glass containers may have graphics applied where the ink provides a graphic design. The ink may also act as a resist for etching the image with acid.

TEXTILES AND GARMENTS

Plastisols and emulsions are the two kinds of inks commonly used to print textiles and garments. Inks based on an acrylic emulsion are suitable for all types of fabric and are printed directly onto it. They will dry at room temperature, but to achieve resistance to laundering, they must be cured 2 or 3 min. at 320°F (160°C). A plastisol is a (dry) vinyl resin dispersed in a plasticizer; there is no solvent. The plastisol is pigmented and printed on the fabric. When heated above 300°F (149°C), the plasticizer "fuses with" the resin and a film is formed. Since the plastisol penetrates the fabric, the film formed on heating incorporates the fabric, producing an excellent bond. Plastisols can also be printed onto release paper, partially cured, transferred to the fabric, and then cured completely.

Plastisol inks must be durable in order to withstand washing and drying of the garment. The cured ink film must remain flexible and adhered to the garment through repeated washings.

QUALITY CONTROL OF SCREEN PRINTING INKS

Because of the exceptionally broad variety of products produced by the screen printing process, a complete discussion of quality control is impractical. As with all inks, color match, color strength, and fineness of grind are important. Adhesion to the substrate, and compatibility with screen, squeegee, and stencil material should be checked. Suitability for the proposed end use is always important.

This is often determined with tests for light resistance, product resistance, weathering resistance, laundering, and the like. Some quality control tests appropriate for screen printing inks are listed in the following table.

Appropriate Quality Control Tests for Screen Printing Inks	
Wet ink film tests	**Dried ink film tests**
Color	Color
Viscosity	Opacity/Hiding Power
Masstone	Rub Resistance
Length	Scuff Resistance
Fineness of Grind	Gloss
Density/Specific Gravity	Adhesion
Tinctorial Strength	Flash Point
Tack	Drying Rate
	Flexibility
	Lightfastness

SUMMARY

The substrate to be printed on is a major cost component in any job to be screen-printed. The interaction of the ink and the variety of substrates to be printed on is complex and difficult to predict without testing for compatibility and performance. Careful and precise discussions among the printer, ink vendors, and substrate vendors can help to reduce the printing problems that may occur during production.

8 PROCESS CONTROL

ll manufacturing processes involve steps leading to a finished product. Each step adds to the total effort required, and every action produces an observable result. Screen printing is no exception. The screen printing process has been studied in order to evaluate numerous process interactions. Tension and fabric, mesh and ink deposit, and stencil and image resolution are just a few screen printing variables that influence process results. This chapter discusses the fundamental principles used in process control and then examines selected screen printing variables that influence process decisions.

QUALITY IMPROVEMENT

The opportunity for quality improvement is always possible. First, the decision to improve the screen printing process must be addressed. The process may then be examined to establish benchmarks for future comparison. Subsequent production analysis will enable comparison of output against current production standards. By using a systematic approach it becomes easy to determine when the process is performing normally and when to take action for correction. The system may also be tested during each step to determine procedures that may "upgrade" output to higher quality levels.

The term *process control* contains two important words. *Process* defines the steps, materials, and all of the actions and components that achieve the goals of production. *Control* indicates how the process functions. Control can be established by first understanding the process through optimization, measurement, and analysis.

Control of the screen printing process or any type of manufacturing requires input to be compared to output. In order to accomplish these objectives, we must have two technologies available: (1) tools to measure the production, and (2) computers to store data and assist in analysis.

George Leyda, GATF research fellow and senior research advisor, suggests the following steps to implement a systems approach for printing that is also applicable to screen printing:

1. *Prepare*—Establish a plan of action. Normalize. Measure.
2. *Analyze*—Examine the data collected to better recognize production capabilities.
3. *Stabilize*—Review procedures.
4. *Optimize*—Ensure operating conditions are appropriate.
5. *Control print*—Run tests/production to meet specified goals.
6. *Control process*—Use measurements to monitor process. Integrate decision trees.
7. *Improve*—Evaluate and review. Revise and implement procedures when necessary to improve process.

Each step of the print process is examined for performance as a discrete component and for interaction with other process steps. Interpretation of the print process characterization data requires careful examination of how the information was obtained and produced; e.g., the printer has to rely on the accuracy and repeatability of the tools and targets.

PROCESS CONTROL TOOLS

Two types of tools will permit the screen printer to use process control to improve quality: (1) mechanical tools used everyday and (2) procedures that ensure precise use of the mechanical tools. Examples of the mechanical tools include tension meters, ink scales, exposure guides, inventory databases, and press tools. Cutters, forklifts, computers, densitometers, and spectrophotometers are examples of auxiliary tools that help in daily production. The procedures are used to be certain the mechanical tools are used properly by all personnel. Procedures are created, documented, and communicated by the screen printer to provide optimal daily production.

Process control tools are used to calibrate the screen printing system. Exposure guides provide verification that a screen

Figure 8-1. Several different types of tension meters. Courtesy Sefar Mesh + Technology

has been properly imaged. Tension meters provide verification that a screen has been properly prepared. Documentation provides a tool for training new personnel or serves as a benchmark for initiating new procedures. Precise use of screen printing process control tools will help in collecting concise data related to process status.

Figure 8-2. Using a tension meter.

PROCESS CONTROL TARGETS

Careful consideration must be used in incorporating print targets during print tests or production work. The targets offer information concerning the capability and status of the printing process. Control targets are integral to every step of the production process, therefore the elements at a minimum are representative of current printing production capabilities. Tint, solid ink and overprint patches, rules, gray balance patches, and impression elements should be present on all print forms. The screen making process will include these elements and should be analyzed to ensure proper screen making. Many manufacturers offer targets for exposure tests.

Each element should be examined for its reproduction quality. Everyone involved in production must be aware of a target's purpose, how to interpret its reproduction quality, and the proper action to be taken following analysis. The procedures developed for operations should include the target's role in normal production.

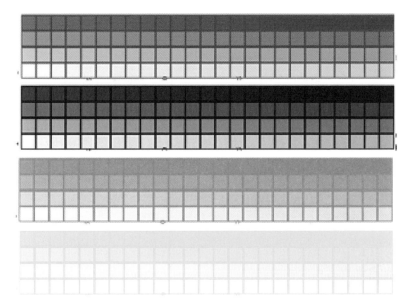

Figure 8-3. Dot percent targets.

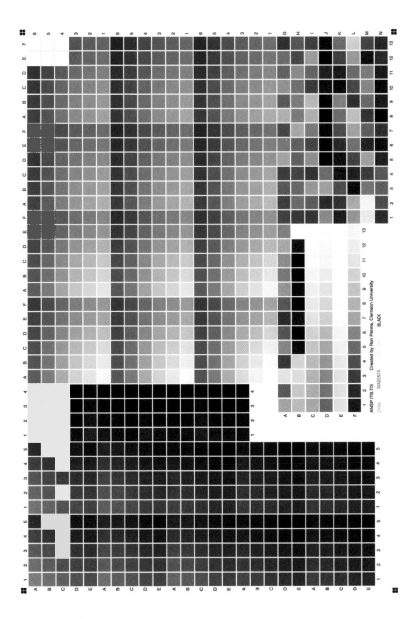

Figure 8-4. The IT8.7/3 target.

PROCESS CONTROL COMPONENTS

All of the materials and equipment mentioned in previous chapters are the components to consider when developing a process control system for screen printing. The impact of one component upon another cannot be understated. Screen printing can reproduce practically any graphic on many different materials. Success depends on the proper selection of screen fabric, frame size, stencil material, ink system, squeegee, and other equipment that will produce the finished image.

A set of production procedures is generalized to present an example of how process control leading to quality improvement can be integrated into production. Simply stated, the objective is to match input to output. The best point to start is carefully considering output: what will the job require? Print tests will establish current capabilities; i.e., how well the components transfer ink onto something. The current system is then compared to the requirements of the job to identify the optimum combination of materials and equipment to use. Predictions on job success can be made from data collected during exposure tests and print tests. Print samples and databases must be used in the evaluation to communicate capabilities. Screen printing presents a large number of variables that will become better understood using these procedures. Stencil and fabric interactions are complex, yet the impact of the squeegee in transferring the ink may blur the image carrier's performance. The small details of screen printing should never be neglected.

SUMMARY

Quality improvement in the screen printing process can be achieved by integrating process control. Perhaps the greatest benefit is gained during development of the system: every component in the current process must be examined by measurement and evaluation. Understanding the optimum performance of the screen printing process will naturally lead to future evaluation of alternative components.

In short, intelligent production decisions are more likely when personnel have learned to think of screen printing as a system.

Developing the system is not inexpensive; monetary and attitudinal investments must be made. Tools must be purchased, and tests must be performed. Training is required, and procedures must be defined. Everyone must pay attention to the small details and how each procedure impacts another: e.g., low mesh tension results in loss of highlight dots and poor tone reproduction. *The screen printing process is a system.*

9 FINISHING

Many screen printing products are not complete after the ink is cured on the substrate. Various processes may be used to enhance or complete the process. Simple cutting operations or complex assembly may be required. This chapter describes some of the options used to complete the process.

SHAPING

The most common finishing operation in graphic screen printing is cutting or shaping the printed piece. Cutters are used to separate multiple images on a sheet and trim excess substrate. Specialized equipment can handle plastic and metal materials. In some cases heated wires may separate vinyl static-cling decals or similar products.

Complex dies may be required to produce shapes that are not square. Dies require additional equipment and a substantial investment. Dies may be made of metal cutting blades mounted on boards. The dieboards may be hand- or laser-cut. The screen printer must know the diecutting requirements beforehand to make sure the image is properly positioned on the substrate. Special locator marks may be printed on the substrate to assist in setup.

SURFACE ENHANCEMENT

Many of the options for surface treatment are available for screen-printed products. These operations include embossing, perforating, and laminating. Embossing produces a raised design on the surface. Embossing requires a two-part die, consisting of male and female components that are pressed together in a platen press or similar device with the substrate sandwiched in between. Perforation strips or wheels cut small holes so the material may be easily pulled apart by the end user. Laminating adheres the substrate to another material to provide stability or meet other product requirements.

Certain products demand more unique surface treatments. Decals for glassware or ceramics must be applied to the product and then heated in a kiln to transfer the print. Heat transfers must be positioned on a garment and transferred by a heat press. Graphics may be embedded during other manufacturing processes, like in-mold manufacturing. Other operations might incorporate hand-applied decorations or etching with acids.

FINISHING CONSIDERATIONS

Since printing may not be the final step in production, several questions must be addressed in planning. First, what will the finishing procedures include? The substrate and printed image may be scratched or the ink scuffed in handling. Heat may deform the product or alter the chemical characteristics of the substrate, the ink, or both. Other stresses may also distort the product, such as

Figure 9-1. Screen presses can incorporate a number of finishing techniques, including coating and weatherproofing.   Courtesy Stork Brabant Inc.

rubbing or chemicals that come in contact with the piece. Screen printers must be sure the ink and substrate suppliers are aware of product manufacturing requirements to prevent unforeseen problems following printing.

Another consideration is the amount of waste present during the finishing operations. Waste allowances, such as for equipment setup, are required in finishing, just as they are in printing. Extra materials must be included so the final product count meets the customer's specifications. Using the techniques described in the chapter on process control should offer insight as to the impact of finishing on production counts.

A third question concerns the amount of time required to complete the finishing operations. Many finishing operations are specialized and are often subcontracted to other companies. Scheduling must be arranged so that product delivery is timely. The client's deadline should be considered, as should the finisher's schedule.

SUMMARY

Finishing adds value to a product. Finishing may enhance a product, or it may be required to add permanence. All finishing requirements must be addressed in initial planning. Specifications for printing will impact the finishing operations and ultimately the success of the job.

10 SCREEN PRINTING INNOVATIONS

E merging technology has impacted all of the major printing processes and introduced nonimpact printing. Offset lithography, flexography, and gravure have experienced shifting markets as a result. Screen printing continues to maintain a modest yet stable share of its traditional markets. New gains are captured by printers who have done their homework by looking at past emerging technologies and finding or creating a fit for future opportunities. This chapter reviews recent innovations in screen printing with a perspective on future trends. Among the topics discussed are digital integration, the World Wide Web, color management, materials and equipment, and productivity.

DIGITAL INTEGRATION

Computers have influenced practically every aspect of human endeavor, and screen printing technology has been influenced as described in earlier chapters. Future innovations will continue to impact screen printing, particularly with large-format printing. Inkjet printing has become an option for short-run large-format products such as specialty banners. As this digital option evolves, screen making may undergo a transition. Increased resolution will provide most graphics printers with techniques for producing imaged screens without film production. Digital files will be proofed by digital devices, and files will then be sent to the screen imaging device. Options for such imaging devices include inkjet resists that form the image. The emulsion is then exposed by a light source. Other techniques will include digitally driven laser devices.

Figure 10-1. Digital technology allows computer-to-screen imaging.
Courtesy FineLine

Digital technology has also influenced traditional techniques of separating color for graphics. Both gray component replacement (GCR) and frequency-modulated (FM) screening techniques are established digital halftoning options. Color palettes used as plug-ins for separations will enable textile and graphics printers to finely tune the films required to produce a multicolor job.

WORLD WIDE WEB

The World Wide Web brings a new dimension to screen printing: communication in a forum open to anyone seeking answers. Answers may be in the form of marketing options, or answers may be for technical questions. As the Web evolves, more files will be sent for proofing and corrections before final proofs and films are required. Transmission technologies will enhance the Web as a tool integrated within a normal production workflow. The greatest benefit has been, and will continue to be, as a source of information: technical expertise will be shared and critiqued in an open environment.

COLOR MANAGEMENT

The language of color communication has reached a common platform of access: measuring tools integrated with software for automating color reproduction processes. Predictable, consistent color is accomplished by following process characterization techniques and using software to provide conversions for color output. Characterization is required in order to fully implement a color management system. Variables must be noted and defined. Computers have made documentation a simple task. Analysis of data used in color management systems is automated by computers.

Figure 10-2. Like all printing processes, color management is an integral part of the workflow as more of the process becomes digital.

MATERIALS AND EQUIPMENT

Stencil, screen fabric, ink, and cleaning systems continue to be modified for better performance. Practitioners continue to study the screen printing process, yielding a better understanding of the

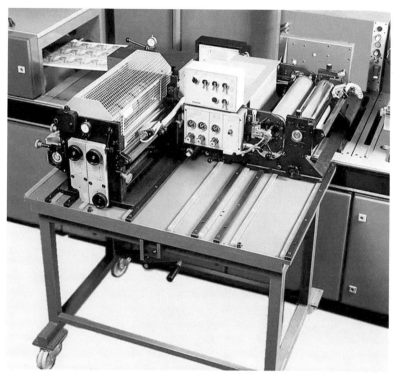

Figure 10-3. Screen printing can be combined with other printing processes to create the finished product. In the press shown above, the press is equipped with a flexo unit and a screen printing unit.

(Below) The em410 press has expansion possibilities of up to 24 interchangeable stations (modular platform contruction), which can be configured from a choice of over 80 different modules. Some of the possible choices include UV and conventional flexographic printing, rotary screen printing, hot foil stamping, embossing, varnishing, and rotary and flatbed diecutting.

Courtesy Gallus, Inc.

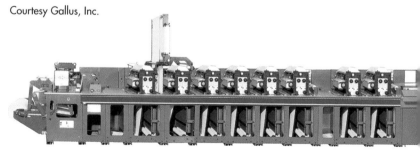

variables. This will lead to innovations improving compatibility in material selection. For instance, emulsions for stencils will be formulated to meet a broader range of quality criteria for imaging, printing, and reclaiming. Improved imaging resolution, better resistance to ink systems, and easier cleaning have seen notable results in recent years. New emulsion technologies include thermal and laser applications.

Screen fabrics may be found in numerous thread counts to fit the most demanding print specifications. Current fabric manufacturing provides high thread counts that were unheard of previously. Printers are measuring tension and learning how higher tension affects the print quality. As demands for print quality increase, screen fabric specifications become critical.

Available ink systems now include UV and water UV in addition to the conventional ink lines already in the market. Demands for lower levels of volatile organic compounds (VOCs) and safer handling keep manufacturers researching for improved ink system components. Color matching requirements and recycling have produced computerized dispensing systems. As color management integrates production workflows, dependable ink systems play a large role in successful color management implementation. The cleaning systems will have to meet the challenges presented by the ink systems, and environmental and recycling concerns are fundamental in future developments.

Presses with automated controls are the result of computer manufacturing innovations. Preset controls assist in press setup, particularly applicable in repeat jobs. Pin registration systems are available for presses as well as screen imaging, meaning less setup time during production. Screen printers have been noted for press innovation due to the nature of the process. Faster, more accurate machines will be the design of the future. Keep a close eye on squeegee and flood bar designs as well. Performance improvement through new profile designs are a possibility as research continues.

PRODUCTIVITY

As the twentieth century draws to a close, a manufacturing paradigm has emerged: requirements for client approval typically include production that is "fast in response, higher in quality, and reduced in cost." Meeting this list of demands appears impossible at first glance. Careful consideration of the tools available will give the knowledgeable printer an edge in competitive markets. Screen printing is a complex manufacturing process. Lack of attention to even a seemingly mundane device such as a squeegee can render a product unusable. Additional productivity enhancers are training, sharing ideas with other printers, and carefully moving forward in linking the components discussed throughout this book.

SUMMARY

Innovation is an ongoing process. Evolution of processes promotes innovation. Print expert and author Mike Bruno points to technology being introduced and merging with existing production processes. Screen printing offers diversity: materials, products, and processes. The presence of diversity often creates innovation. The opportunity to excel depends on the screen printer's desire and creativity to evaluate new technologies and effectively plan for change. A solid foundation in the basic components of the screen printing process will foster understanding current techniques and integration of new technology.

Glossary of Terms

Abrasion Resistance The inherent ability of a surface to inhibit deterioration or destruction by friction. Also called *rub resistance.*

Absorbency The ability of a paper or other porous substance to soak up the liquids (e.g., the vehicle in an ink) and vapors (e.g., moisture) with which it comes in contact.

Additives Ingredients added to printing ink to give special characteristics or properties.

Angle of Attack In screen printing, the position of the face of the moving squeegee blade and the plane of the screen under pressure. Because the blade is flexible, the angle of attack differs from the squeegee angle, which is measured without movement or pressure.

Automatic Feeder A device for picking up single sheets from a pile and moving them, one at a time, into the printing area of the press.

Binder A component of the vehicle of printing ink that holds the pigment to the printed surface.

Blockout In screen printing, a liquid masking material used to cover non-image areas of the screen around the perimeter of the stencil. It seals the fabric of the printing screen against leakage in the nonimage areas between the design and the extreme edges of the printing frame.

Bottle Press A screen printing press capable of printing on cylindrical or other three-dimensional shapes.

Carbonized Thread Monofilament screen fabric threads that have been treated to prevent the buildup of static electricity through friction during screen printing.

Carousel A multicolor screen printing device that typically has multiple platens that rotate around a central shaft.

Ceramic Ink An ink containing ceramic pigments and flux that is applied to a ceramic substrate by screen printing.

Clamshell Press A flatbed screen printing press designed with the screen carriage (frame) hinged to the printing table at one end.

Colorant An ink, pigment, toner, or dye that modifies the natural color of a substrate.

Color Sequence The order in which colors are printed on a substrate as indicated by the order in which inks are supplied to the printing units on the press. Color sequence determines how well the inks will trap on the substrate.

Color Strength The relative amounts of pigment or other colorant in an ink.

Comprehensive A detailed sketch, done in the final step of the design process, which should closely resemble the finished product.

CONDUCTIVE INK   An ink for the screen printing of electronic circuits containing materials that permit an electric current to flow through the printed line or pattern.

CONTACT FRAME   A device that holds the imaged and photosensitive materials together for exposure in contact photography.

CONTINUOUS-TONE COPY   An image with differing tonal values or shades, such as a photograph.

COPY   Artwork and text.

CURING   The conversion of a wet ink film to a solid ink film.

CYLINDER PRESS   In screen printing, a press that consists of a screen carriage, squeegee, and impression cylinder, used to print flexible substrates that can be attached to the cylinder.

DECAL   A design screen-printed on a special paper for transfer to a substrate. Pressure-sensitive markings and water-slide transfers are two examples of decals that are externally processed before application to the end-product.

DIRECT STENCIL   A light-sensitive liquid emulsion that is squeegeed into the screen fabric and becomes a stencil when contact exposing and processing are done on the screen.

DIRECT/INDIRECT PHOTOSTENCIL   A combination of an indirect film stencil and direct emulsion.

DOUBLE-X SYSTEM   A system used to measure multifilament mesh. The XXs are preceded by number that provides an indication of the fineness of the fabric. The higher the number, the finer the mesh and the smaller the mesh openings. 6XX has about 74 threads per inch, and 25XX has 196 threads per

inch, but these exact counts vary slightly from manufacturer to manufacturer.

DUROMETER   A value used to measure the hardness of a squeegee blade. Durometer increases with hardness.

EMULSION   A solution that contains light-sensitive diazo or bichromate compounds used in the direct stencil method in screen printing.

EVAPORATION   A process by which most screen printing inks dry. The liquid solvents evaporate into the air, leaving the pigment adhered to the substrate.

EXTENDERS   Substances added to printing ink to reduce the cost of the ink or to change its consistency.

FADE RESISTANCE   The ability of a printed substrate to resist deterioration (e.g., fading and yellowing) caused by sunlight or artificial light. Alternative term: *lightfastness.*

FILM POSITIVE   A photographic reproduction, on a film base, with the same tonal values as those of the original image.

FLATBED PRESS   A press used to print flat substrates. The substrate is placed on a flat table or bed to keep it stationary during printing.

FLEXOGRAPHY   One of the major printing processes. Employs a flexible rubber or photopolymer plate that has the image areas in relief (i.e., raised) above the nonimage areas. Used primarily to print products for the packaging industry.

FLOCK   Finely cut fibers of fabric that are adhered to a substrate for decoration.

FLOOD COAT   An even coating of ink, which covers the surface of the screen but is not forced through the image areas, to insure proper ink supply to all parts of the screen during impression.

FRIT   A smelted mixture of soluble and insoluble materials form a glass that when quenched in cold water shatters into small friable pieces. Used in glass colors and overglazes.

GLAZE   A thin vitreous coating, either colored or clear, that attaches itself to the body of ceramic ware, imparting a gloss and smoothness to the surface.

GRAPHIC ARTS CAMERA   A camera used in the graphic communications industry, designed to photograph flat copy such as photographs, artwork, and type.

GRAVURE   A printing process that uses an image carrier in which the image is engraved or etched below the nonimage surface. The image carrier is coated with ink, with the excess ink being scraped off. The inked image is transferred to paper or another substrate by contact.

HAIRLINE REGISTER   A standard for accuracy in which the maximum deviation between printing colors is 0.003 in. (0.08 mm), which is approximately equivalent to one-half row of dots in a 150 line/inch halftone image.

HALFTONE   Tone values represented by a series of evenly spaced dots of varying size and shape, the dot areas varying in direct proportion to the intensity of the tones they represent.

HAND TABLE OPERATION   Screen printing operation done manually with manual feed and squeegee operations.

HAZE   The residue of ink and/or stencil material remaining in a screen following stencil removal. Often requiring caustic detergents for complete removal.

HIGHLIGHT   The lightest or whitest area of an original or reproduction, and represented by the densest portion of a continuous-tone negative and by the smallest dot formation on a halftone and image carrier.

INDIRECT FILM (TRANSFER FILM)   A light-sensitive gelatin emulsion coated on a polyester or plastic carrier sheet that is exposed to a film positive and chemically processed into a stencil before being adhered to the stretched screen fabric. After the stencil is dry, the carrier sheet is removed. (Knife-cut stencil films are also considered transfer films.)

INFRARED DRYING UNIT   A system consisting of a canvas or wire mesh conveyor belt that carries the freshly printed substrate through a drying section of infrared lamps and reflectors.

INK SETTING   The first step of oxidative drying, where the solvents contained in the vehicle evaporate, leaving the drying oil and pigment.

INTAGLIO   See *gravure*.

JET DRYER   A system consisting of a canvas or wire mesh conveyor belt that carries the freshly printed substrate through a drying section of high-velocity hot air.

KNIFE-CUT STENCIL   A stencil, cut by hand from paper or film, normally used to produce bold lines and solid areas.

LEADING   The amount of extra space between lines of type.

LETTERPRESS   A printing process that utilizes raised (relief) images as the printing image carrier.

LINE IMAGES   Solid areas with no shading or tones, including type, drawings, and diagrams.

LITHOGRAPHY   A method of printing from a plane surface (a smooth stone or metal plate) on which the image to be printed is ink-receptive and the non-image area ink-repellent.

Long Inks   A term used to describe printing inks that pull away in strands when touched. Long inks are used in printing processes when the ink must be transferred from roller to roller.

Masking Film   A knife-cut film that can be cut and peeled in positive form, consisting of a translucent or transparent support layer coated with red or amber emulsion that absorbs specific wavelengths of radiation.

Mesh   The open space between the woven threads of screen printing fabric through which the ink passes during printing.

Mesh Count   The number of openings per linear inch in any given screen printing fabric. The higher the number, the finer the weave of the screen fabric.

Mesh Opening   In screen printing, a measure of the distance across the space between two parallel threads, expressed in microns.

Monofilament   A single strand of synthetic fiber that is woven with others to form a porous screen fabric.

Multifilament   Many fine threads twisted together to form a single thread of synthetic fiber that is woven with others to form a porous screen fabric.

Off-contact Printing   Screen printing done with the screen lowered to a point slightly above the substrate. The squeegee is drawn across the screen with downward pressure, pushing the stencil into contact with the substrate.

On-contact Printing   Screen printing done with the underside of the screen in full contact with the substrate.

One-man Squeegee   A squeegee that is mounted on a counter-balanced carrying device so that the operation of very large squeegees can be accomplished with a minimum of effort.

Open Stencil   A stencil that transmits an inked image in the shape of a cutout by holding it tightly against substrate and brushing ink, paint, or other colorant through the cutout.

Overlay   Tissue or frosted or clear acetate or Mylar, holding elements such as surprints, knockouts, or overlapping or butting flat colors, that is attached to a pasteup.

Oxidation   A slow chemical reaction of the reactive drying oil of printing ink with oxygen to produce a dry ink film.

Pasteup   The assembly of all copy elements in their finished form on heavy stock such as bristol board.

Penetration   A process of ink drying by which the ink is absorbed into the substrate, which sets the ink. The solvent then evaporates, leaving the pigment and hardened binder on the substrate.

Photolettering   Type that is produced by arranging film positives on the camera copyboard and photographing the arrangement.

Photostencil   A stencil in which image and nonimage areas are produced photographically.

Pica   A unit of measuring type in the point system. Six picas measure close to an inch, and there are twelve points in one pica.

Pigments   Solid coloring particles derived from natural or synthetic sources used to give color to printing inks.

PLAIN WEAVE A pattern of weave in which fabric threads are woven one over and one under, as opposed to twill weave whereby threads are woven over one and under two.

PLASTISOL A dispersion of finely divided polyvinyl chloride resin or resins in a plasticizer or series of plasticizer.

POLYESTER A thermosetting plastic that is capable of being drawn into very fine strands that can be woven into many types of textiles, including screen printing fabrics.

POINT The smallest unit for measuring type in the point system. A point measures 0.0138 in. (0.35 mm). With the advent of desktop publishing, the point is now usually considered to be ½ in.

POINT SYSTEM A method used by the graphic communications industry for measuring type.

POLYMERIZATION A chemical reaction between the binder and the solvent of printing ink, leaving a tough and hard ink deposit.

PRESENSITIZED FILM An indirect film that is light-sensitive from the manufacturer.

REGISTER MARKS Small reference patterns, guides, or crosses placed on originals before reproduction to aid in color separation and positioning negatives for stripping. Register marks are also used to aid in color register and correct alignment of overprinted colors during printing.

RESIN Solid or semisolid organic substances used as a binder in a printing ink.

ROTARY SCREEN PRESS A screen printing press utilizing a fine-wire cylindrical screen, which a contains squeegee-like

blade inside, that rotates over a continuous web of paper.

ROTOGRAVURE A printing process that uses a printing cylinder with the image etched below the nonimage surface in the form of tiny sunken cells. The cylinder is immersed in ink, and the excess ink is scraped off by blade. When paper or other substrates come in contact with the printing cylinder, ink is transferred.

SAWTOOTH A notched effect where the lines in a design cross the fabric mesh of the screen printing screen diagonally, distorting the design contours.

SCOOP COATER A tool for coating screen printing fabrics with photosensitive emulsions for making photostencils.

SCREEN FABRICS Woven webs of materials (natural or synthetic fabrics and fine wire) used as image carriers in screen printing.

SCREEN PRINTING A printing process in which ink is forced through a porous open-mesh screen that has nonimage areas blocked out in some manner and image areas left open to permit the flow of ink through the screen.

SCREEN RECLAMATION The process of stripping the stencil from the screen so that a new stencil can be applied.

SCREEN RULING The number or dots or lines per linear inch in a halftone screen image.

SEMIAUTOMATIC FLATBED PRESS A flatbed screen printing press in which sheet feeding and removal are manual but in which the actual printing operation is automatic.

SERIES An assortment of many type sizes in one design.

SERIGRAPHY A fine art screen-printed reproduction of an original artwork.

SHADOW The darker or denser areas of an original, film positive, or halftone reproduction.

SHORT INKS Inks that do not pull away in long strings when touched, but rather break in short peaks (similar to the consistency of soft butter).

SOLVENT A component of the vehicle in printing inks that disperses the pigment and keeps the solid binder liquid enough for use in the printing process.

SQUEEGEE A rubber or plastic blade, attached to a handle, used to force ink through the open areas of the stencil and mesh to the substrate.

SQUEEGEE ANGLE The angle formed by the near-vertical axis of the squeegee and the plane of the screen, measured when the squeegee is in position but no force or pressure has been applied. See also *angle of attack*.

STENCIL A material, which is adhered to the screen, that blocks the screen mesh to keep ink from reaching the substrate, thereby creating nonimage areas.

SUBSTRATE Any base material that can be printed or coated.

TENSION METER A precision instrument used to measure the surface tension of the stretched screen fabric.

THUMBNAIL SKETCH One of several basic sketches made in the early design stages to explore different layout ideas.

TYPE Standardized forms of letters, characters, and punctuation marks.

TYPEFACE Name of particular standardized form of letters, characters, and punctuation marks.

TYPESETTING The operation of assembling types into words and lines in accordance with the manuscript and typographic specifications.

ULTRAVIOLET CURING UNITS A conveyor that carries the printed substrate under a focused beam or area of reflected ultraviolet light, drying the substrate by the curing process.

ULTRAVIOLET (UV) INKS Printing inks containing a photoinitiator that when exposed to an ultraviolet radiation source causes polymerization of the monomers and oligomers in the ink.

UNSENSITIZED FILM An indirect film that must be made light-sensitive prior to its use.

VEHICLE The liquid portion of ink that contains solvent and binder.

WARP The lengthwise direction of threads in a woven fabric.

WEFT The horizontal threads or fibers that cross the warp at a right angle.

WICKET DRYERS A series of lightweight metal racks, which hold the printed substrates, mounted on a moving conveyor belt. Wicket dryers are used for drying flat or sheet-type substrates.

INDEX

ABOUT THE AUTHOR

Dr. Samuel T. Ingram is a professor of Graphic Communications at Clemson University, where he has been a faculty member for thirteen years. He received his undergraduate degree from Appalachian State University in 1978. He was granted his Doctorate from Clemson University in 1985.

His primary responsibilities at Clemson are teaching, research and interaction with the printing industry. Dr. Ingram teaches all printing processes with special focus in color reproduction, color science, process control, and workflow. He has held membership in a number of technical and trade associations, including the Technical Association of the Graphic Arts, Graphic Arts Technical Foundation, Screen Graphics and Imaging Association, Gravure Association of America, Flexographic Technical Association, International Graphic Arts Education Association, and Southeast Prepress Association. Dr. Ingram has served a term on the board of directors for TAGA and numerous technical committees in other organizations, including the United States Technical Advisory Group. He received the Mentor Award from the Screen Printing Association International (now SGIA) in 1988.

Dr. Ingram's research in color measurement, color management systems, and print process modeling continues. His interest in new technologies remains active, particularly through participation in research efforts, and his enthusiasm for teaching continues to grow. He can be reached at **sting@clemson.edu**.

ABOUT GATF

The Graphic Arts Technical Foundation is a nonprofit, scientific, technical, and educational organization dedicated to the advancement of the graphic communications industries worldwide. Its mission is to serve the field as the leading resource for technical information and services through research and education.

For 75 years the Foundation has developed leading edge technologies and practices for printing. GATF's staff of researchers, educators, and technical specialists partner with nearly 14,000 corporate members in over 65 countries to help them maintain their competitive edge by increasing productivity, print quality, process control, and environmental compliance, and by implementing new techniques and technologies. Through conferences, satellite symposia, workshops, consulting, technical support, laboratory services, and publications, GATF strives to advance a global graphic communications community.

The Foundation publishes books on nearly every aspect of the field; learning modules (step-by-step instruction booklets); audiovisuals (CD-ROMs, videocassettes, slides, and audiocassettes); and research and technology reports. It also publishes *GATFWorld,* a bimonthly magazine of technical articles, industry news, and reviews of specific products.

For detailed information about GATF products and services, please visit our website at *http://www.gatf.org* or write to us at 200 Deer Run Road, Sewickley, PA 15143-2600. Phone: 412/741-6860.

GATF*Press*: Selected Titles

- **Understanding Digital Color**
  by Phil Green

- **On-Demand Printing:
  The Revolution in Digital and Customized Printing**
  by Howard Fenton and Frank Romano

- **Glossary of Graphic Communications**
  compiled by Pamela Groff

- **Professional Print Buying**
  edited by Phil Green

- **Handbook of Printing Processes**
  by Deborah Stevenson

- **Flexography Primer**
  by J. Page Crouch

- **Gravure Primer**
  by Cheryl Kasunich

- **Lithography Primer**
  by Dan Wilson

- **On-Demand & Digital Printing Primer**
  by Howard M. Fenton

- **The GATF Encyclopedia of Graphic Communications**
  by Frank Romano and Richard Romano

- **A Short History of Printing**
  by Frank Romano and Peter Oresick